BRITTANY

THE HELM FRENCH REGIONAL GUIDES

Series Editor: Arthur Eperon

Auvergne and the Massif Central
Rex Grizell

The Dordogne and Lot
Arthur and Barbara Eperon

Languedoc and Roussillon
Andrew Sanger

The Loire Valley
Arthur and Barbara Eperon

Provence and the Côte d'Azur
Roger Macdonald

Forthcoming:

South West France
Andrew Sanger

Normandy
Barbara Eperon

Paris
Vivienne Menkes

BRITTANY

Frank Victor Dawes

Photographs by Joe Cornish

CHRISTOPHER HELM
London

© 1989 Frank Victor Dawes

Photographs by Joe Cornish
Line illustrations by David Henderson
Maps by Oxford Cartographers

Christopher Helm (Publishers) Ltd
Imperial House, 21–25 North Street,
Bromley, Kent BR1 1SD

ISBN 0-7470-0611-3

A CIP catalogue record for this book is
available from the British Library

Typeset by Tradespools Ltd, Frome,
Somerset
Printed and bound in Italy

Contents

Acknowledgements

With many thanks for the assistance, information and advice generously offered by Toby Oliver of the Brittany Ferries Information Bureau and by the staff of the Comité Régional de Tourisme.

BRITTANY

1
Introduction

Brittany. *Bretagne. Breiz Izel.* Whether you say it in English, French or native Breton, there are few place names that evoke such a warm response from so many people. At the mere mention of it, *Monsieur Hulot's Holiday* comes to life, with thoughts of shrimping nets, those miniature rakes and all the other *Articles de Pêche* together with buckets and spades, mats and parasols.

This long nose of France jutting out into the Atlantic remains essentially what the Romans called it, Armorica, or 'land of the sea'. Flying up from Rio de Janeiro this, and the Channel Islands just beyond, is the first sight of land after eleven hours of seemingly empty and endless ocean. From this lofty perspective the bravery of the corsairs such as René Duguay-Trouin, who captured Rio from the Portuguese in 1711 and after whom one of the *bassins* of St. Malo harbour is named, can be properly appreciated. They roved the sea for months on end without a sight of land and for centuries the island of Ouessant (Ushant in English), off the tip of that 'nose' or promontory, was their landfall returning home; for the rest, a check on their position as they made course up the English Channel. Even today the deepwater fishing fleets from ports such as Lorient, Concarneau and

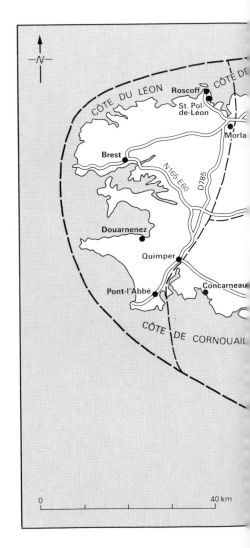

Douarnenez range as far away as Senegal in their search for sardine, mackerel and tuna.

The salt wind from the sea is a constant reminder of Brittany's heritage. medieval architects allowed for it by filling their church steeples as full of holes as a pepperpot and the country wives put gaps in their tall lace caps for the same reason. This wind-battered peninsula is a large one, as big as Denmark, a country in itself. It roughly parallels its smaller English cousin 200km or so to the north, and with its lighthouses and lobster pots, its coves and creeks where boats lie high and dry at low tide, its broad sands and seaweed-covered rocks filled with secret pools, its tradition of cider making, it is indeed reminiscent of Devon and Cornwall.

Part of the southern coast is called Cornouaille. This is Cornwall with a

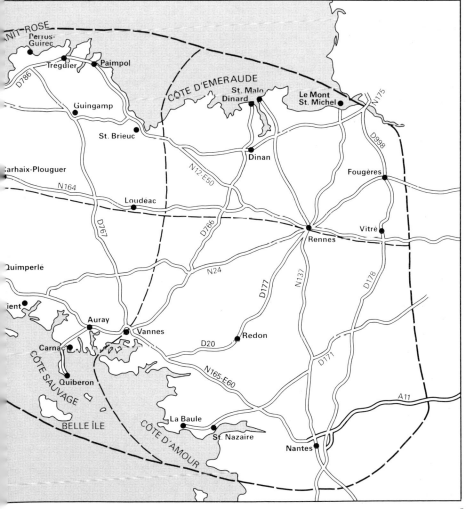

French accent, though some of the inhabitants still speak the Breton tongue which prevailed up to the 10th century and which to this day, or so your guide will claim, can be understood by Welsh speakers. Whether this be true or not, Breton is one of the six Celtic languages along with Welsh, Gaelic, Irish, Manx and Cornish, and this fact allies Brittany genetically closer to these nations than to the rest of France. Politically and economically, though, it is very much a province of that country. The sight of a woman in the *pays* Bigouden astride a buzzing black Solex motor scooter, head down to keep her tall white lace *coiffe* in position, seemed to me a vivid illustration of these contrasting strands in Breton life. Brittany is as French as a *baguette*, a packet of Gauloises Blond cigarettes or that umbrella on wheels the Citroën 2CV—and at the same time as Celtic as bagpipes and cider.

Today, access for the family motorist to Brittany is easier than ever with regular sailings by Brittany Ferries from Portsmouth to Caen and St. Malo and from Cork and Plymouth to Roscoff. For those who prefer to fly, there are direct links between Britain and various airports in the province such as Lorient, Rennes, Brest and Dinard. But the latest improvement in communications between Brittany and the rest of Europe is on the railways. In 1989, SNCF extended its high-speed TGV network to the far west of France. It is now possible to travel on the silver, blue and white TGV Atlantique at 300km/h from Paris to Connerré on its own dedicated track and at 220km/h on branch extensions from there to Rennes and Nantes using conventional track. The journey time from Paris is reduced to two hours —less than the onward journey takes to

Quimper or Brest. Another innovation is a weekly Motorail service linking Boulogne and Nantes. When the Channel Tunnel comes into service the whole TGV network will be linked to British Rail.

Brittany is surrounded on three sides by that natural boundary, the sea, and its coast remains its greatest natural asset: a thousand kilometres of it, indented with gulfs, bays, harbours and countless secluded coves and beaches. Twice in recent years it has been despoiled by major oil spillages from supertankers. When the *Torrey Canyon* went aground off the Scillies in 1967 the tide brought quantities of stinking black tar ashore on the coasts of Brittany as well as Britain. Worse was to come. In March 1978 another supertanker, *Amoco Cadiz*, was wrecked on the Finistère coast itself, disgorging a quarter of a million tonnes of oil, with correspondingly even greater damage to the environment. Plant and wild life has only now recovered from this appalling disaster, which it is to be hoped will never recur.

It is often claimed that Brittany is at its best in May and early June, or even in October, but it is essentially summer holiday country. Many of the hotels and restaurants, and even some of the smaller resorts, shut down completely from October to May. If you are driving to the southern coast of Brittany from St. Malo or one of the Channel ports through what is known as La Haute Bretagne, Upper or High Brittany, it is a pity to dash past some of the marvellous walled towns, châteaux, forts and

The head-dress of the pays Bigouden *can't be missed*

4

battlemented abbeys which can be reached with a few short detours.

Mont St. Michel, geographically, is in Normandy but it serves as a northern gateway to Brittany, its unmistakable silhouette breaking the flat horizon of the marshes. It is worth visiting once, despite the almost overpowering crowds it attracts into its confined spaces. Much quieter and hardly less dramatic are the fortified towns of Fougères and Vitré, reminders of the feudal lords who once held the frontiers between Brittany and the rest of France. At Redon the canal dreamed up centuries ago to link Nantes and Brest inland (thus avoiding the British fleet offshore) intersects with the River Vilaine via locks at either side. This is the crossroads of Brittany's waterways, an attractive town, somewhat marred by the heavy road traffic which rumbles and trundles through it ceaselessly. By contrast, the mysterious bog of the Parc de Brière, a short drive southwards, is deserted save for a few reed gatherers, peat cutters, fishermen and duck shooters. It can be explored only by chaland propelled like a punt with a long pole by the boatmen guides.

This fascinating place lies just behind the great shipyards of St. Nazaire, busy with the construction of a new generation of big ocean-going passenger liners and car ferries, and the splendid beaches of La Baule, Le Croisic and a string of smaller, beguiling resorts, not least of which is St. Marc-sur-Mer, just south of Pornichet, where Jacques Tati filmed Monsieur Hulot's Holiday in the 1950s. Since then, in a reorganisation of local government throughout France in the 1960s, this entire département (Loire-Atlantique, formerly Loire Inférieure)

was transferred en bloc from Brittany to a newly created administrative region, the Pays de la Loire. Its historical and cultural links, as an integral part of La Haute Bretagne, with La Basse Bretagne to the west, seemed to count for little with the planners. Nor did the fact that its main city, Nantes, was the ancient capital of Brittany. But although such roots have little interest to bureaucrats, they can hardly be ignored in a guide book such as this. It seems poetically just that the extension of the TGV rail network to South West France should perpetuate the role of Nantes as the gateway to Southern Brittany.

As far as this author is concerned, Brittany still consists of five départements rather than the four to which it has been officially reduced. In this book, Loire-Atlantique forms—with Ille-et-Vilaine—La Haute Bretagne, the buffer state, as it were, between bretonnant (Breton-speaking) Brittany and the rest of France. The three départements of the the west: Morbihan (which in Breton means 'Little Sea'), Finistère (simply, 'Lands End') and Côtes-du-Nord ('North Coasts') are La Basse Bretagne. To many people, both native and visiting, the latter is the real Brittany, where the Breton language and Celtic culture is kept alive despite all the pressures of late 20th-century living.

But to complicate matters, the traditional frontier between High and Low Brittany doesn't correspond to the departmental boundaries—it lies more or less along an imaginary line between St. Brieuc, capital of the Côtes-du-Nord, and Vannes, capital of Morbihan, and that is the boundary adopted by this guide. Westwards lies the 'Little Britain' of the Celtic migrants from Cornwall and Wales. The further west you go through Morbihan, Côtes-du-Nord and Finistère, the more apparent becomes the innate Breton character of the people and the architecture and the granite which has shaped them both. Because most visitors congregate on the coasts, the interior of Brittany, the Argoat, tends to be neglected and accommodation can be found without having advance booking even at the height of the summer season. Yet it, too, can offer the tourist a diversity of sights and experiences. Argoat means 'Land of Woods', a misnomer these days when so much of the Breton landscape seems to consist of endless fields of artichokes, cauliflowers and sunflowers. Brittany Ferries began as a company shipping vegetables, mostly artichokes and cauliflowers from the 'golden belt' of the Ceinture Dorée, across the Channel before branching out into the profitable business of transporting tourists as well.

Inevitably, modern, mechanised farming has swept away much of the old Breton *bocage* system of small fields hemmed in by earth banks planted with trees and hedges of wild hydrangea, leaving the open country cruelly exposed to the winds that tear in from the Atlantic. What woods have survived the relentless advance of the tractor and the plough are places of enchantment, rustic glades of oak and beech filled with music of rushing streams, the wind whispering the legends of Merlin and the Lady of the Lake. There are wide stretches of open heath where the granite protrudes in fantastically shaped boulders and outcrops through the thin layer of soil and where heather and gorse bloom purple and yellow in season. Narrow roads wind between high earth banks. There are commanding

hills but no true mountains.

Superstition is embedded in the land like the granite, outwardly expressed in the megaliths found all over Brittany. Ankou, the Coachman of Death, still stalks the wild countryside where that ever present wind tears at the thatch of the stone cottages and farmhouses. Breton religious fervour is expressed in granite, too, in innumerable small churches, shrines and calvaries and in the remarkable *enclos paroissiaux* (parish closes) consisting of a cemetery, an ossuary or charnel house, a triumphal arch and a calvary surrounded by carved stone saints and martyrs. Brittany is of course noted for its *pardons*, the name for an annual religious festival honouring a local saint. They mostly take place in country towns or villages during the summer months. If you have a chance to visit one, don't miss it. Apart from the Mass, with hymns in the Breton language, usually held outside in the church grounds, you will see a procession with local people dressed in the traditional lace *coiffes* and embroidered *chupen*. The religious ceremonies are accompanied by fêtes, fairs and folk dances with stalls selling cider and hot buttered *crêpes* made on the spot. At some places long trestle tables covered with cloths or paper are set up in the churchyards for the serving of *ragoût à la mode de chez nous* to the accompaniment of the *biniou* and the *bombarde*, the Breton versions of bagpipes and oboes.

Breton folk music has undergone a tremendous revival in recent years. It is largely instrumental and has more in common with other Celtic countries such as Ireland, Wales and Scotland than with other French regions, although the *bombarde* relates it also to

Spain and North Africa. The Breton national anthem *Bro Goz Ma Tadou* has the same meaning and tune as the Welsh *Land of My Fathers*. Brittany, however, does not go in for massed choirs; as with the Scots, the skirl of the pipes has a dramatic effect on its expatriates. As well as *pardons*, Brittany has its secular festivals, of which the best known is the week-long Fêtes de Cornouaille, held annually in Quimper at the end of July. This has become a gathering of Celts from all over the world, somewhat after the fashion of the *eisteddfod* of Wales. Concarneau has its Fête de Filets Bleus, which takes its name from the blue fishing nets which are hung along the approaches to the Ville Close, the walled town overlooking the harbour. It started as a ceremony of blessing the nets to guarantee a good catch but has grown into a full-scale festival held every August on similar lines to the Fêtes de Cornouaille.

If you are touring rather than staying in one resort, a 10- to 14-day visit to most of the major centres and other places of interest will cover around 1,600 kilometres. A good road map is essential if you intend to explore the by-ways: I use the Michelin Road Atlas and the whole province is covered to a scale of 1:250,000 in No. 5 of the *Institut Géographique National Carte Touristique*. A more leisurely way of touring on four wheels, without despoiling the environment in any way, is by horsedrawn caravan or *roulotte*. There are companies in Finistère, Morbihan and Ille-et-Vilaine who will arrange tours of a weekend, a week or more in a caravan for four people with cooking facilities. Cycling is a healthy and economical way of seeing the country—500km spread over a couple of weeks is a not too demanding tour—and bikes travel free on most cross-Channel ferries. Alternatively, it is very easy to hire a bicycle in Brittany.

For those who prefer Shanks's pony, Brittany is a walkers' dream with numerous long distance trails around the coasts and into the Argoat, marked out and listed by the *Comité National des Sentiers de Grande Randonnée*. Route GR34 retraces the Tro-Breiz, the ancient pilgrimage around Brittany's cathedrals, covering over 800km. On a less ambitious scale most of the local Syndicats d'Initiative can supply maps of local footpaths and landmarks.

Not surprisingly, Brittany attracts many yachtsmen to its harbours and marinas on the coast and boat trips to the numerous offshore islands are extremely popular with visitors. It is sometimes forgotten that the inland waterways of Brittany offer an opportunity to explore the countryside, including parts which are rarely visited by tourists, in various types of craft from canoes up to 28-metre barges as luxuriously equipped as a 4-star hotel.

Most sports are catered for, apart from fishing and watersports. Facilities for tennis and riding have expanded rapidly and golf looks like being the growth sport of the 1990s. A few years ago there were only 50 courses in the whole of France—now there are three times that number, and some of the finest are in Brittany. Useful addresses and telephone numbers will be found in the Practical Information section at the end of this book, as well as the dates of *pardons* and festivals, lists of tourist offices, museums, châteaux and recommended restaurants and hotels.

Like everywhere else in Western

Europe, Brittany is changing to keep pace with the late 20th century. No longer is it a quaint backwater known to the authorities in Paris mostly for its bloody-mindedness. The days of barricades bristling with artichokes in persistent disputes about the price of vegetables now belong to the past.

The Bretons are a deeply conservative race but *crêperie* franchises and theme parks are moving in. Autoroutes and major hotel chains such as Ibis and Novotel have arrived. For all that, Brittany is still characterised by the modestly priced, family-run small hotel or restaurant. Standards of accommodation vary widely. Although many establishments now provide facilities such as toilet and shower *en suite* they can often be blatantly do-it yourself installations decorated with horrendous selections of wallpaper. A listing by *Logis de France* is a reliable indication of good value and a mention in the red *Michelin Guide* is a guarantee of quality, especially if a restaurant is included.

Apart from hotels and *auberges*, youth hostels, *gîtes* and 800 well-equipped campsites are to be found in abundance all around the coast and inland as well, where they are less likely to be fully booked in peak season. As far as beach space is concerned, there is more than enough for all unless you must go to La Baule or Dinard during the French school holidays and pay 5F for an ice cream cornet. A consolation though for parents is that these larger resorts offer 'Mickey Clubs' on the beach with trampolines and organised games to keep the children occupied all day.

GLOSSARY

aber—estuary (as in Wales)
andouilettes—sausages
auberge—inn
bagne—prison
biniou—bagpipe
bisquine—oyster smack
bocage—system of hedged fields
bombarde—Breton oboe
bragou braz—wide breeches
bretonnant—Breton speaking
brocante antiques
calvaires—religious monuments
chaland—flat-bottomed boat
chupen—embroidered velvet waistcoat
cidre bouché—flat cider
coiffe—lace head-dress
cotriade—fish stew
crêpe—pancake
criée—fish auction
crosse—primitive hockey
dégustation—tasting
enclos paroissiaux—parish enclosure
faïenceries—glazed pottery
far—pudding
festou noz—night festival
galette—pancake
gîte—self-catering cottage
giz folk dress
goat—**(also coat,goët,hoët)** —a wood
goëmonniers—seaweed gatherers
haras—stud farm
kenavo—goodbye
korred—elves
lit-clos—box-bed
matelote d'anguille—eel stew
mortas—bog oak
palet—Breton quoits
pardon—annual religious festival
porte triomphale—triumphal arch
roulotte—caravan
'Royale'—the Navy
traou spont—events foretelling death
tro Breiz—tour of the Seven Saints' cathedrals
Yermat—'Your Health'

Conversion Tables

km	miles	km	miles	km	miles
1	0.62	8	4.97	40	24.86
2	1.24	9	5.59	50	31.07
3	1.86	10	6.21	60	37.28
4	2.48	15	9.32	70	43.50
5	3.11	20	12.43	80	49.71
6	3.73	25	15.53	90	55.93
7	4.35	30	18.64	100	62.14

m	ft	m	ft	m	ft
100	328	600	1,968	1,500	4,921
200	656	700	2,296	2,000	6,562
300	984	800	2,625	2,500	8,202
400	1,313	900	2,953	3,000	9,842
500	1,640	1,000	3,281	3,500	11,483

ha	acres	ha	acres	ha	acres
1	2.5	10	25	100	247
2	5	25	62	150	370
5	12	50	124	200	494

kg	lbs	kg	lbs
1	2.2	6	13.2
2	4.4	7	15.4
3	6.6	8	17.6
4	8.8	9	19.8
5	11.0		

°C	°F	°C	°F	°C	°F
0	32	12	54	24	75
2	36	14	57	26	79
4	39	16	61	28	82
6	43	18	64	30	86
8	46	20	68	32	90
10	50	22	72	34	93

2
History

Thousands of years before Caesar came, saw and conquered, or before the monks driven from Cornwall and Wales by the pagan Northmen crossed the English Channel with their Christianity and boatloads of immigrants, a civilisation existed on the Armorican Massif that was part of the Hercynian Fold thrown up from beneath the sea by a mighty geological convulsion *five hundred million years ago*. The granite outcrops of Brittany are among the oldest rock to be found on the face of this earth. The standing stones and dolmens, or burial chambers, fashioned from that rock which was ancient even then, are the only clues remaining of the Megalithic tribes which inhabited this land 1,500 to 3,000 years before the birth of Christ.

Certainly, these monuments were there and were prehistoric when Julius Caesar arrived in 56BC to conquer the westernmost promontory of the Gauls which they called Armor 'Land of the Sea' and Argoat 'Land of the Woods' for the interior. This region had been occupied since the 6th century BC by the various Gaulish tribes of the Curiosoliti, Osismi, Namnetes, Redones and the Veneti.

The Gauls settled five areas which roughly correspond to the five *départements* of Brittany drawn up after the Revolution of 1789. The Redones were centred at Rennes, the Namnetes at Nantes and the Veneti at Vannes—and it is worth noting that all these names survive, as does Morbihan (Little Sea), which the Veneti dominated from their capital on its shores.

After the capture of the promontory Caesar's admiral, Brutus, showed no mercy, in fact. The Veneti leaders were summarily slaughtered and the entire tribe sold into slavery. Although the memory of the invader's iron fist survives in Roman text and Breton folklore, little remains above ground of the occupation and civilisation of Armorica, the Latin version of Armor, which lasted four centuries until it was abandoned by Rome and torn apart by the barbarous Franks.

The next milestone in the long history of this settled but somehow untameable region comes during the Dark Ages, after the Roman legions had pulled out of Britain, leaving it to the mercy of raiders form the Continent and the north. Armorica was by then the all but forgotten furthermost province of Rome. During the 5th and 6th centuries, for some 150 years, its lonely shores received successive waves of migrants from the western parts of the British Isles: Celts who fled from the Norse and Danish raiders of the eastern

11

coasts of England and were finally driven out altogether. They were led by their monks and holy men, seven of whom became founding saints of bishoprics in their adopted home which they renamed *Breiz Izel*, Little Britain, or in French *la petite Bretagne*.

Brittany is said in legend to have seven thousand, seven hundred, seven score and seven saints: which when set down as a precise mathematical total of 7,847, seems somewhat improbable. Be that as it may, the names of villages and small towns throughout the province commemorate, in common with similar places in Wales and Cornwall, the names of otherwise forgotten saints such as Cadoc and Columb, Donat and Devotus, Merryn and Miliau and many, many others (see page 14).

Rather like squatters, the new people arrived with their different language, customs and religion and simply took over Armorica. They brought with them, too, their superstitions and legends that combined Christianity and witchcraft, angels and demons, fairies and wizards. The folklore of Brittany and Britain is inextricably entwined with stories of King Arthur's knights searching for the Holy Grail in the Forest of Brocéliande, where Merlin, the king's wizard and spellbinder, fell under the spell himself of the fairy Viviane, the Lady of the Lake, while he slept. The glades of this medieval hunting ground are haunted still by these ghosts although the forest is today known as Paimpont.

Île Tristan, off the southern coast of Brittany, is named after Tristan, the legendary Celtic hero, whose love for Isolde inspired Wagner's opera, which opens with the couple sailing from Brittany to Cornwall. It is claimed that King Mark of Cornwall had a palace at Douarnenez near the island which he presented to Tristan. It is said, too, that the bells of the submerged city of Ys can still be heard ringing beneath the Bay of Douarnenez.

Two centuries after the mystic Celts crossed the English Channel with their Christian faith and their pagan myths and legends to found a new homeland in their 'Little Britain', Charlemagne, King of the Franks and ruler of most of western Europe, was crowned Emperor of Rome by Pope Leo III on Christmas Day 800. Charlemagne conquered Brittany without too much difficulty but as the Chinese proverb says 'You can conquer a country on horseback but you have to dismount to rule'. Charlemagne decided to hand over responsibility for ruling the strange Breton breed to a local, Nominoë, whom he dubbed Count of Vannes. Later Nominoë was made first Duke of Brittany by Charlemagne's last surviving son, Louis.

But it was not enough to satisfy Nominoë's ambition. He raised Dol, the most respected of the Breton bishoprics, to the status of Archbishopric. He had no intention of remaining under Frankish rule and demonstrated this on the death of Louis by leading a Breton army to victory over Charles the Bald at Redon in 845, one of the most important dates in the history of Brittany. Nominoë had himself crowned king of an independent Brittany in the cathedral at Dol. He did not survive long enough to defend and nurture his little kingdom, constantly under attack and harassment by Vikings who had settled in Normandy.

After 50 years of incursions from Normandy, Duke Alain Barbe-Torte ('Alan of the Curly Beard'), a youth of only 20 at the time, finally at Questembert in 937 succeeded in driving out the invaders who had ranged the coast in their dragon-headed longboats killing, pillaging and terrorising. The city of Nantes, so readily accessible on the River Loire, had suffered especially and Duke Alain set up his capital there, despite the rival claims of Rennes. The Duchy lasted for six centuries, which has gone down in Breton history as a 'Golden Age', although not without challenge from within and without.

No sooner had Duke Alain died than the nobles whose châteaux he had fortified against the Normans began denying the right of his heirs to govern them and warring with each other. William the Conqueror's subjugation of Britain in 1066 left Brittany in an awkward position between Normandy and the new kingdom across the Channel, and a century later Duke Conan IV allied himself to Henry II of England, marrying off his daughter to a son of the Plantagenets. When the son of this union, Arthur, was murdered by King John in 1203 in case he became a contender for the throne of England, Arthur's half-sister, Alice, and her French husband, were given the opportunity to found a new dynasty of Dukes of Brittany.

Another century passed (in relative peace) until the death in 1341 of Duke Jean III began another of the more or less constant battles and struggles for succession, the bloody 'War of the Two Jeannes', so called because the wives of the two contenders bore that name. The heir apparent, Charles of Blois, was married to the duke's niece Jeanne de Penthièvre, whose brother Jean de Montfort, married to Jeanne of Flanders, was the rival. So the stage was set for a family struggle that grew into a war, with the King of France supporting Charles and the King of England siding with the de Montforts.

Bertrand du Guesclin, a grim-visaged but gallant knight whose fame is remembered throughout Brittany, although not always kindly, earned his spurs in this War of Succession in the service of Charles of Blois. Born in a castle just outside Dinan in the area that was loyal to Charles and his Jeanne, du Guesclin held the town against the English. During more than two decades of this power struggle for control of Brittany, he never wavered in his determination to keep the English on the opposite side of the Channel, despite being taken prisoner and treated as a guest, albeit an enforced one, at the Court of King Edward.

The War of Succession culminated in the Battle of Auray in 1364 with defeat of the House of Blois. Charles was killed and du Guesclin taken prisoner and ransomed by the English for 100,000 crowns. Although England appeared to have backed the winner in the de Montforts, with a new young Duke Jean IV in power in Brittany, France was the eventual beneficiary. Released from captivity, du Guesclin went on to serve the new King of France, Charles the Wise, with an army known as the *Grandes Compagnies* in battle after battle, becoming Constable (Commander-in-Chief). Throughout his military career he directed his efforts to driving the English out of France and he died fighting them at Châteauneuf-de-Randon in the Massif Central in 1380, but in his own homeland of Brittany he was vilified as a traitor for having marched against Duke Jean on the orders of the king. As recently as 1946 his statue at Rennes was blown up by Breton nationalists.

The history of Brittany during this turbulent period has to be studied in the wider context of the Hundred Years'

7,847 Saints

The Celts who migrated from western Britain in the 5th and 6th centuries were led by their monks and holy men, seven of whom were the founders of bishoprics in their adopted home which they renamed *Breiz Izel* (Little Britain). These seven were so revered that they became unofficial, uncanonised saints—the *Septs Saints Fondateurs*—Brieuc, Corentin, Malo, Patern, Paul-Aurelian, Samson and Tugdual. In medieval times the *Tro-Breiz* was a tour of Brittany visiting the cathedrals of all seven. They are the first division of an ecclesiastical league numbering seven thousand, seven hundred, seven score and seven saints: or 7,847!

Despite, or perhaps because of the wonderful variety and richness of the religious life in this one province of France

Kant bro, kant giz
Kant pariz, kant iliz

'a hundred countries, a hundred guises, a hundred parishes, a hundred churches', Breton saints tend to specialise. St. Vio makes the rain fall (or stops it), St. Herbot heals sick animals, St. Cado looks after soldiers and St. Efflam consoles conscripts. Female saints have their place: Ste. Barbe offers protection from thunder and lightning and Ste. Gwenn, depicted with three breasts, looks down with special favour on triplets.

War which began in 1337, when Edward III of England laid claim to the throne of France, and includes the battles of Crécy, Poitiers and Agincourt as well as the Black Death. After Agincourt, England seemed to have the upper hand for a time until Joan of Arc intervened as kingmaker. As intrigues and war continued between the opposing sides separated by the Channel, Brittany remained determined to keep itself independent of France, although union of the two was inevitable. The future Duke of Brittany, Arthur III, foreshadowed this when he united with his King to drive the English out of France and bring the Hundred Years' War to an indeterminate end.

One of his successors, François II, kept Henry Tudor (the future King Henry VII) and his uncle imprisoned for nearly 14 years when they escaped to Brittany during the civil wars between their House of Lancaster and the House of York. The Wars of the Roses ended with the Battle of Bosworth in 1485 and just three years later François fought his own last battle against the French crown at St. Aubin-du-Cormier. He was roundly beaten, his Breton army routed, and had no option but to sign a treaty with Charles VIII under which none of his daughters could be married off without the consent of the king. Three weeks later he died of despair, to be succeeded by his 11-year-old daughter Anne, destined to become the best remembered and revered ruler of Brittany (see page 18). To this day it is hardly possible to travel through the province without encountering some reference to La Bonne Duchesse, la petite Brette or one of the other various attractive titles she acquired.

Place Names

Place names in Brittany contain a wealth of meaning and historical significance, if only one knows a few basic words to be able to interpret them. Basil Cottle devotes a section of his fascinating study *Names* (Thames and Hudson) to Brittany and a more detailed guide is to be found in the *Dictionnaire Entymologique des Noms de Lieux en France* compiled by A. Dauzat and C. Rostaing.

While some of the larger towns, such as Rennes, Nantes and Vannes, derive their names from the Gaulish tribes who were conquered by the Romans, the majority of smaller towns and villages were named by the Celtic settlers from Britain. In some cases, a French rendering has obscured the original Breton, so that Kemper (confluence of rivers) becomes Quimper, Konk-Léon (bay of Léon) is now Le Conquet and Konk-Kernev—the bay of Cornouaille, named after Cornwall—is known as Concarneau.

The most obvious thing to a visitor from Britain is the similarity between certain place names or prefixes and those encountered in Wales, especially Lan or Lam (Llan in Welsh), which in both cases means 'Church of'. Thus Lannion and Lampaul means the churches of SS John and Paul respectively. Although the 'Lan' part is easy to spot, it isn't always so easy to match the saint correctly. Lanildut and Lannedern identify Illtyd and Edeyrn (whose church at Llanedeyrn is very near Cardiff). Langolen has a familiar ring to it and Lanrivan could be St. Ruan, who crops up again and again in Cornwall.

St. Kay, who was steward of King Arthur's Court, has left his name in Cornwall, too, and this is transported to Brittany at St. Ke, frenchified on some maps as St. Quay. And what of Landudal, Lanriec and Lanurvan? They may, or may not, refer to SS Tudal, Rioc and Urbain. Lan may also be a reference to a holy place or religious community, as in langoat. Goat, coat, goët, hoët mean 'a wood'. Thus, holy place in a wood.

The influence of the church is seen in a variety of other prefixes and suffixes: Loc or lok, which also means 'sacred place' and Plou, ploe, plo or pleu (a parish). Ker means house or village, tre or tref is a hamlet, and gwik, gui or guic a town or borough. So Locmaria, Kermaria and Locmariaquer are variously St. Mary's place, village and the two combined in one. Guimiliau, with its gorgeous parish enclosure, is named after St. Miliau, a 6th-century prince, as is Ploumiliau. Lampaul-Guimiliau pairs St. Paul and St. Miliau.

Not every place name in Brittany has a holy or religious connotation, however. Kerfourn boasts a furnace, Kerfeunteum a spring, and Kermoroc'h a porpoise. Plougastel-Daoulas, where a famous liqueur is produced from the local strawberries, means 'a castle parish' with 'black stream' after the hyphen—the same that occurs in the name of Douglas and in various other spellings as a place name (Dulas, Dowlais, Dawlish) throughout Britain.

The Welsh connection recurs with the name for estuary 'Aber' in the far West—Aber Wrac'h, and two more named after saints, Aber-Ildut (Illtyd again) and Aber-Benoît (Benedict). Enez, the Breton word for island, sounds not unlike the Welsh ynys. Ménez (mountain) is mynydd in Welsh. Perhaps it isn't so surprising after all that Breton fishermen have been known to claim that taking shelter from a storm in a Welsh port they had little difficulty in making themselves understood.

Anne was not yet 15 when she married Charles VIII of France; but Charles died after seven years and their four children all died in infancy. Anne returned to her beloved Brittany before marrying the new King of France, Louis XII, as she was obliged to do by treaty. But they had no sons and, when she died at 36, her eldest daughter Claude inherited the Duchy.

The end of Brittany's independence was in sight. When Claude married the future François I in May 1514, Brittany was part of the dowry and she died ten years later after bequeathing the Duchy to the Dauphin François. In 1532 a meeting of the States of Brittany at Vannes sent François a request for an Act of Union, which was granted and published at Nantes on 13 August.

Although in theory the edict of François promised to respect the Bretons' traditional rights in accordance with Duchess Anne's wishes, in practice after the ending of the golden age of the Duchy, Brittany never again knew independence. Nor did it know peace. The Wars of Religion brought terror even to remote villages, while the Catholic Duke of Mercouer plotted to take over the province. He was prevented by the people appealing directly to the King, Henry IV, a Protestant turned Catholic. He turned the tables on the Catholic League by going to Nantes in 1598 to sign the Edict granting religious freedom to the Huguenots, thus making Protestantism legal in France.

There was also the tyranny of the tax collector. In Duchess Anne's time the States of Brittany had the power to levy their own taxes. Following union with France taxes were imposed from Paris and under Louis XIV became excessive and greatly resented in Brittany. This led in 1675 to the revolt of the *Bonnets*

Rouges which was put down by the French army and the Rennes *parlement* suspended. Although that peninsula of the far west was by now firmly established as a part of the great kingdom of France, its name seemed synonymous with rebellion and disaffection. In 1764, twenty-one years ahead of the start of the French Revolution, the Breton parliament revolted against the power of the Crown, expelled the Jesuits for their intrigues and dogmatism and gained the support of the parliament in Paris.

Brittany at first welcomed the storming of the Bastille on 14 July 1789 as the end of royalty and autocracy. But by January the following year the name of Brittany had disappeared from the map to be replaced by five *départements* in line with the division of the entire country drawn up in Paris. Moreover, the taxes imposed by the Republican Government and the laws passed against the Church and its priests speeded the process of disillusionment. The execution of King Louis XVI in 1793 goaded the Breton anti-revolutionaries, the Chouans, into action under the banner of 'Vive le roi, vive la bonne religion'.

A royalist 'invasion' at Carnac in 1795 under the protection of British warships was rapidly defeated and resistance against the Republicans collapsed. Like General de Gaulle in 1940, Georges Cadoudal, leader of the Chouans and royalists in Basse Bretagne, fled to England and became commander-in-chief in exile. Unlike de Gaulle he did not return to victory but to a firing squad after trying to kidnap Napoleon.

A Breton warrior who fared much better under the new régime was Theophile-Malo Corret, better known for his adopted name of La Tour d'Auvergne, which has been applied to streets, squares and public buildings throughout the land. Bonaparte named him 'First Grenadier of the Armies of the Republic' and awarded him a sabre of honour (see Box in Chapter 5). Brittany produces men of action as well as artists, thinkers and writers; and the military tradition continues at the St. Cyr army officer school at Coëtquidan on the edge of the forest at Paimpont and at the strategic naval bases of Brest. Men like La Tour d'Auvergne, who combined literary and military qualities, are rare. Pierre Abelard (1079-1142) who was born at Le Pallet in Muscadet wine country between Nantes and Clisson, achieved immortality for the story of his love for Heloise, 'the wise Heloise for whom he was castrated and became a monk at Saint-Denis', rather than for his teaching of heretical theology (see Box in Chapter 5). Alain-René Lesage (1668-1747), author of *Gil Blas* and a native of Vannes, rates as one of the province's major playwrights and novelists; and also in the 17th century Père Albert Le Grand of Morlaix enhanced Breton literature with his scholarly chronicle of Breton saints *Les Vies des Saints de la Bretagne-Armorique*. Madame de Sévigné, whose letters give a vivid picture of 17th-century life in Brittany, lives on in spirit at the Château Les Rochers a few kilometres south of Vitré (see Box in Chapter 4). The 19th century brought further literary recognition of Brittany through the work of Chateaubriand, and who can say what inspiration Jules Verne obtained from his home city of Nantes when he later went to Paris to write his particular combination of travel tales and science fiction?

During World War II, the whole province was occupied by the Germans. Brest, Lorient and St. Nazaire were important bases in the battle of the Atlantic and Hitler ordered the construction of concrete fortifications around the Breton promontory as part of his Atlantic Wall. These works were on a scale that dwarfs the prehistoric megaliths and are still very much in evidence 45 years after the war ended. The Germans had expected to be greeted as liberators in Brittany, releasing its people from the French yoke which they had reluctantly suffered since the Union of 1532. Instead they ran up against an underground Resistance as determined and ruthless as anywhere else in France, if not more so.

By 1944 the end of Occupation was in sight and came that August with unexpected speed. General Patton's army, pushing south from the Normandy beachheads, liberated Brittany in two weeks—save for pockets of German resistance in some of the major ports. Brest, Lorient and St. Nazaire suffered tremendous damage and were almost totally rebuilt after the war with scant regard to history. However, the old city within the walls of St. Malo, which had been shelled and bombed to rubble, was recreated in its original medieval pattern with a skill and faithfulness that demands respect.

Unlike other parts of France, the history of Brittany is not expressed in soaring Gothic cathedrals but in smaller churches and chapels with beautiful medieval woodwork and painting and intricately carved stone calvaries; not in rich palaces filled with old masters and fine furniture but in solid granite fortresses and grey-slated towns where the heart of Brittany beats slow and strong, undisturbed by passing time and fashions.

Duchesse Anne de Bretagne (1477–1514)

It is impossible to travel very far in Brittany without encountering some reference to the lady who ruled it as an autonomous state towards the end of what many Bretons feel was their Golden Age. The Duchess Anne was crowned as an 11 year old in Rennes Cathedral on the death of her father Duke François II, who had struggled in vain against the ambitions of the rulers in Paris to make the dukedoms of Burgundy and Brittany part of the kingdom of France. He had just fought and lost a crucial battle against the French at St. Aubin-du-Cormier and had been forced to sign a treaty with Charles VIII under which none of his daughters could be married off without the consent of the king.

There was nothing particularly unusual in the late Middle Ages about a child being put in a position of regal authority and even at her tender age when she became Duchess, Anne seemed equal to the task and no mere puppet of her advisers and courtiers. In fact, she soon fell out with them over a scheme to marry her off to a 50-year-old Breton nobleman, Alain d'Albret, whose complexion was as foul as his temper. At 13 she was married by proxy to Maximilian of Austria, besieged and then courted by Charles VIII of France, who at 21 was much nearer her own age and skilled at tennis, hunting and jousting. He contrived to have the proxy marriage annulled and made her his own Queen (as well as being Duchess of Brittany) before she reached the age of 15.

A year or so later the Venetian ambassador wrote a graphic description of the young couple in a despatch from Paris: she small, thin, visibly lame in one foot 'although she uses a false heel' and very determined for her age; he also small and ill-formed with an aquiline nose much out of proportion to the rest of his face, slow of speech. Despite their apparently unprepossessing appearance they seemed happy together, but the marriage was not a long one; Charles died after seven years from an accidental blow on the head and the four children she bore him all died in infancy.

Anne married the new King, Louis XII, as she was obliged to do by treaty, at the Château of Nantes in 1499. The terms of the marriage contract were more favourable to Brittany than those of her previous marriage and Louis gave Anne a pet name of '*ma bretonne*'. He left the governance of the Duchy to her. These were triumphant times for Brittany. On a tour of the Duchy in 1506, she received the plaudits of her people wherever she went. At Brest she named the flagship of the French fleet *La Cordelière* which went on some years later to trounce Henry VIII's ships in a fierce battle off Ushant before going down in flames.

Yet for all her popularity, Anne suffered repeated setbacks in her efforts to secure the succession in Brittany's favour. When her first child by Louis, little Claude, was two, she betrothed her to the grandson of Maximilian of Austria but Louis in retaliation made a will that Claude should marry the heir to the French throne, François d'Angoulême. Anne's only hope of keeping Brittany out of the clutches of France was to produce a son to inherit the dukedom. She had two, both stillborn, before giving birth to a second healthy daughter. Then early in 1514, weakened by repeated confinements and fever, she became ill and died at the age of 36.

The funeral procession from the Château of Blois, where she died, to Paris took more than a week and was arranged with the utmost pomp, accompanied by hundreds of torch-bearers and horses draped in black velvet, with the Brittany Herald-of-Arms in the van, carrying her crown. Vigil was kept in churches along the route where her body rested during the hours of darkness and she lay in state for two days in Notre Dame in Paris before the funeral at St. Denis, the last resting place of French monarchs. Her heart was buried in a golden casket in the cathedral at Nantes. Anne had been twice Queen of France but had never wavered in her love for her own Breton people and the cause of Breton independence, which, alas, died with her despite all her efforts on its behalf.

Les Bonnets Rouges

When Cardinal Richelieu established a naval dockyard at Brest and felled the forests of the peninsula to build new ships he began a policy of asset-stripping that was continued in Louis XIV's reign with punitive taxes on the people. A new tax on *papier timbré*, the stamped paper on which official documents were written, and on tobacco and pewter ware, led to a revolt which began in Bordeaux in March 1675 and swiftly spread to Rennes, where tax offices were sacked. No sooner had this been put down, than trouble broke out in Nantes and St. Malo. The King, furious at the Breton trouble-makers, sent a force to punish them. But summary executions and the threat of a salt tax (*gabelle*) failed to prevent riots spreading to Basse Bretagne, where peasants calling themselves the *Bonnets Rouges* rioted in the streets and marched on châteaux with church bells ringing, to drink the cellars of the *seigneurs* dry. Some historians see it as the first rumblings of the French Revolution more than a hundred years later.

Sebastien Le Balp, a Carhaix lawyer, assumed leadership of the *Bonnets Rouges* and planned to occupy Morlaix and hand it over to a Dutch fleet in the Channel. Thirty thousand peasants sacked Carhaix and set it on fire but Le Balp was killed and without him the revolt collapsed. Terrible reprisals followed, with mass hangings and burning of houses. The Breton Parliament was sent packing from Rennes to Vannes while a virtual army of occupation descended on the province, looting and raping.

3
Food and Drink

Food

It comes as no surprise that the Gauls' and the Romans' 'land of the sea' specialises in seafood. Indeed, the most famous lobster dish of all is *homard à l'Armoricaine* in honour of Armor or Armorica, although some authorities insist on calling it *á l'Americaine* on the grounds that it was invented by a Parisian restaurateur for an American customer. (Another version is that it was created from a family recipe by a young Breton who opened a restaurant in America, from whence it was exported to Paris under its fashionable new name.)

My own preference is for the former title and indeed the finest lobster I have ever tasted was caught off the coast of Morbihan, brought live to the kitchen of the Hôtel-Restaurant Hubert in Erdeven, where it was killed and grilled in tarragon, the speciality of M. Hubert, the proprietor (see *Recipes*). It was preceded by *foie gras Périgord*, followed by the cheeseboard or *le Plaisir des Îles* (ice cream flambéd in Armagnac) and washed down with Chablis per cru Domaine Jaboulet.

This was part of the normal lunchtime service of a 2-star Logis inn in a small grey village that one might drive through without a second glance. Just as our modestly priced dinner menu the previous evening in a similar establishment at Peillac, a village on the Nantes-Brest Canal outside Redon, had included a half lobster grilled in sauce Antoine, ray poached in Bernaise sauce and other delectable seafoods, as well as steak, lamb or veal. As in other areas of France, the sauces make the meal, and the Breton chef produces a distinctive flavour with a *beurre blanc*, using cream and butter mixed with wine, vinegar and shallots. There is, too, a cold sauce quite often served instead of mayonnaise, using butter instead of olive oil, which is quite delicious with salads and cold fish. Stuffed clams (*palourdes*) and mussels (*moules farçies*) and *feuilleté* pastry bulging with shrimps, crayfish or mussels, are a feast to remember in themselves.

The freshness of such a variety of foods that cost so much more elsewhere is a temptation to forget about dietary restrictions and tuck in with wild abandon. Apart from lobsters, there is an abundance of langoustes, langoustines, scallops (the best of which come from St. Brieuc, Quiberon Bay or Brest), prawns, shrimps, cockles and mussels, not to mention sardines, mackerel, tunny and salmon. Supermarkets also stock very good fish soup in jars, such as that made from Guingamp langoustine,

20

fresh salmon is relatively inexpensive and some have water tanks from which you can catch your own live crab or lobster. The Breton version of the Provençal *bouillabaisse*, called *cotriade*, makes good use of these ingredients in a memorable stew. Eel stew (*matelote d'anguille*) is also a regional speciality and the best eels come from the Grande Brière, that great brooding marsh just inland from St. Nazaire.

Another seafood that can be prohibitively expensive in other places is affordable here: the Breton oyster. Despite the rule about only eating them when there is an 'R' in the month, freshly harvested oysters can be tasted live without risk during the summer season in Brittany and no *gîte* can be considered as fully equipped if its kitchen lacks an oyster knife, with its short triangular blade and a hand guard to protect you from the sharp shell. There are two simple ways of making sure that an oyster is alive before you swallow it whole: either touch the dark edge of the flesh with a knife or let a drop of lemon juice fall on it and the ciliary fringe will give a noticeable twitch. There should be some water in the shell when the oyster is opened.

Seafood isn't by any means the whole story of Breton cuisine. Sheep bred on the salt pastures of the coast provide a meat called *pré-salé* which when served with white beans becomes a delicacy. Pig farming is of great importance in Brittany. Morlaix is celebrated for its ham and sausages, whether the *andouille* of Guémené-sur-Scorff or the *andouillette* of Quimperlé, memorable for quality and taste. Nantes, like Aylesbury, is celebrated for its duck, Rennes for its chickens and the Vilaine and Brocéliandé for geese. The Breton *dindonneau* or young turkey makes a succulent

alternative to chicken and *magrit de canard aux pommes*, duck fillets cooked with apples, is highly recommended.

As for fruit and vegetables, the promontory grows enough superb cauliflowers, globe artichokes, onions and turnips and other early season vegetables for its own needs as well as for export, and these are an important part of the regional cuisine. The quality of the soil and the mild climate also produce such fine fruit as the strawberries of Plougastel-Daoulas and, more surprisingly and less well known, the melons of Rennes known as *petits gris*.

Nor is a sweet tooth underrated in Brittany, where almost every town seems to make its own particular kind of biscuits, cakes and sweets and you will find them displayed on supermarket shelves in attractive tins and packages with pictures on: butter cake called *kouign aman* and *gâteau brestois* with almonds, lemon and Curaçao, the raisin *galettes* of Vannes and the *petites galettes* of Pont-Aven, Playben and Trégastel, the *crêpes dentelles* of Quimper, crisp thin rolled pancakes, the *brioches* of Morlaix, the *perlingots* of Nantes, the caramels of Rennes, and so on.

Finally, it is impossible to write about food in Brittany without mentioning *crêpes*. The Breton will eat them, accompanied by *cidre bouché*, a flat cider served in a brown pottery cup, as a kind of 'high tea'. A savoury pancake topped with a lightly fried egg, will be followed with others filled with jam or honey or sweet apple. The *crêpe bretonne* comes as paper-thin *crêpes dentelles*, buckwheat *galettes*, *crêpes au blé noir* made from black wheat, *tomha-ynn*, a crêpe filled with ice cream and chocolate sauce, flambéd in Calvados. The variety seems endless and there are *crêperies* everywhere.

21

Recipes (Compiled and tested by Kate Dawes)

All recipes serve 4, except where otherwise indicated.

It is usual at Brittany's markets, folk festivals or fairs accompanying the annual *pardon* to see crêpes being turned out by the dozen on the heavy open air *galettières*. It seems so easy as the *galettier* skilfully spreads the thin batter with a special wooden rake and spatula but the novice at home or in a holiday *gîte* needs a lot of practice to achieve the same results. There is no secret formula to Brittany crêpes but a confident touch is required. The recipe below has proved the most successful for me.

Basic breton Crêpes
INGREDIENTS

75 g plain flour	150 ml milk and water
25 g buckwheat flour	good pinch salt
2 medium sized eggs	clarified butter, oil or lard
30 ml melted butter or oil	for greasing

METHOD
Sift flour and salt into a bowl, beat eggs and stir them into flour with melted butter or oil. Stir gently until smooth, gradually add milk and water. Leave to stand for 2 hours or as long as convenient.

Choose frying pan heavy enough to disperse heat yet light enough to handle. Heat pan then grease it, for each crêpe spoon 45 ml into hot greased pan. Tilt pan so that batter thinly coats the surface. Cook over medium heat for 1 min until bubbles start to form underneath, slip a spatula around the edges, turn crêpe over and cook for 1 min. Stack crêpes as they are made and keep warm over a pan of hot water.

For sweet crêpe add 25 g sugar to basic recipe. Variations of fillings are endless: try seafood in a creamy sauce, ham and mushroom, or cottage cheese, tomato and finely chopped fresh herbs. Crêpes keep well in the refrigerator, so are an excellent standby.

Raie en Beurre Noir (skate in black butter sauce)
INGREDIENTS

1–2 skate wings cut into three or four serving portions	2 tablespoons capers
	5 tablespoons fresh chopped parsley
1 litre court bouillon	45 ml wine vinegar
25 g butter	seasoning

METHOD
Wash fish well, put into a deep frying pan, cover with court bouillon. Heat to boiling point and simmer for 10 to 15 min. Lift out fish—drain and gently scrape away skin. Keep hot in ovenproof dish. To make black butter—pour off stock, put butter in frying pan and heat until rich golden brown colour. Spoon quickly over fish, season with salt and pepper, scatter over capers and chopped parsley. Add vinegar to pan, heat quickly and pour over fish. Serve at once.

Breton sauce

INGREDIENTS

2 level tablespoons Dijon mustard	45 g unsalted butter
2 egg yolks	salt and freshly ground black pepper
1 tablespoon wine, cider or tarragon vinegar	2 tablespoons chopped parsley and chives

METHOD

Beat mustard, egg yolks and vinegar together until well blended, season with salt and black pepper. Put butter in a bowl over pan of hot water and stir until softened (not melted). Gradually add butter to egg mixture beating all the time, until sauce has consistency of thick cream, stir in finely chopped herbs. Breton sauce is reminiscent of mayonnaise but is easier to make and less oily. The sharp flavour of the sauce makes it a perfect foil for cold mackerel, trout or herring.

Humbler varieties of fish such as whiting, eel and mackerel are often relegated to the stewpot for the local fish stew—*cotriade*. Tradition has it that *cotriade* began as a sailors' stew boiled up on board from any unwanted part of the catch.

Cotriade
(fish stew with sorrel and leek)

INGREDIENTS

750 g rich fish	
750 g white fish	2 leeks, chopped
1 litre fish stock	2 cloves garlic, finely chopped
800 ml mussels	bouquet garni
300 ml canned or cooked sorrel	salt and pepper
60 g butter	300 ml double cream or crème fraiche
500 g potatoes	6—8 croûtes fried in butter then rubbed with garlic
2 onions, chopped	

METHOD

If using eel, skin and fillet it. Fillet the fish and use the heads, tails and bones of all the white fish to make fish stock. Cut the fish fillets into 5 cm pieces, wash and dry them. Clean the mussels. Quarter the potatoes and slice them thinly. In a large pot heat 30 g butter and cook the onions, leeks and garlic 2—3 min until soft not brown. Add the fish stock, bouquet garni, salt, pepper and potatoes and simmer for 5 min until potatoes are slightly cooked. Add the rich fish, simmer gently for another 3—4 min. Add the white fish, simmer for 5 more min. Add the sorrel, the mussels in their shells and the cream. Continue simmering for 3 min or until mussels are opened. Taste for seasoning, discard the bouquet garni. Serve *cotriade* with croûtes fried in the rest of the butter.

23

Beurre Blanc Nantais
(white butter sauce)
INGREDIENTS (makes 250 ml)

3 tablespoons white wine vinegar	2 shallots, very finely chopped
3 tablespoons dry white wine	250 g very cold butter salt and white pepper

METHOD
In a small pan (not aluminium) boil the vinegar, wine and shallots until reduced to 1 tablespoon. Cut the butter into small pieces, set the pan over a low heat and gradually beat in the butter, a piece at a time, to make a smooth creamy sauce. Work sometimes over low heat and sometimes off the heat so that butter softens and thickens without melting. Season to taste with salt and pepper. Serve as soon as possible.

Brittany has retained a taste for outmoded puddings, known in Breton as *fars*. The most famous of all is *far breton* which resembles a Yorkshire pudding flavoured with prunes or raisins, and is baked in a shallow dish so that the crust is crisp. All *fars* are substantial fare calling for a hearty appetite.

Far Breton
(prune flan)
INGREDIENTS

125 g prunes	125 g sugar
125 g flour	2 eggs
600 ml milk	1–2 tablespoons rum

METHOD
Soak the prunes in a bowl of hot water for 2 hours until soft then drain them well. Butter a 2-litre baking dish thoroughly and spread the fruit in the baking dish. Set the oven at moderate heat (180°C, 350°F, Mark 4). Sift the flour into a bowl and make a well in the centre. Add the milk and lightly whisk in the flour until mixed (strain if there are any lumps). Add the sugar, eggs and rum and stir to a smooth batter. Pour the batter over the fruit and bake in a heated oven for 1 1/2 hours, or until well browned and dry when tested with a skewer. Cut the flan like a pie into wedges or squares and serve lukewarm. Dark raisins often replace the prunes in *far breton* to make *far aux raisins*. Soak them in the rum for 30 min, drain them well and use the fruit and rum as in this recipe.

Breton lobster
(serves 2)
Lobsters are no longer readily available in Brittany, most are consumed in restaurants and hotels. If you should want to cook a very special dish I recommend this recipe as served by M. Hubert in his hotel at Erdeven.

INGREDIENTS

1 Breton lobster (800 g)
2 shallots
30 g butter
2 tablespoons tarragon
   vinegar

$^1/_2$ teaspoon curry powder
30 g crème fraîche
whisky and armagnac to
   flambé
15 g grated cheese

METHOD

Cut the live lobster in two lengthways. Heat through in a large pan with butter, finely chopped shallots and tarragon vinegar. Flambé with whisky and armagnac. Lift out the two pieces of lobster and keep hot. Reduce the pan juices, stir in and cook curry powder, add crème fraîche and blend well together over a moderate heat. Pour sauce over the lobster, sprinkle with grated cheese. Cook in the oven for 12 min at 350°F (180°C, Mark 4).

The Oysters of Brittany

If oysters are your thing, the best place to sample them in the whole of Brittany is at Cancale on the bay of Mont St. Michel, a town wholly devoted to their *dégustation*. The most expensive are the *véritables Cancales*, otherwise known as *pieds de cheval* because they are shaped like a horse's hoof. The *plates*, or flat oysters, are called *Belons* after the estuary near Quimperlé in the south which used to dominate the *ostreiculteurs'* trade, along with l'Armoricaine from Concarneau and Île-Tudy. These days oysters are bred on the sheltered southern coast before being shipped north to places like Cancale and Morlaix to grow to maturity.

In her book, *The Oysters of Locmariaquer*, the American writer Eleanor Clark describes in detail and with great affection the long and hard process of oyster cultivation and its history from the viewpoint of one Morbihan fishing village: 'Intimations of the ages of man, some piercing intuition of the sea and all its weeds and breezes shiver you a split second from that little stimulus on the palate.' Fresh oysters of the same kind that the Roman legions prized are still cultivated around the Gulf of Morbihan and at Belon and Kerfavy-les-Pins, as well as around the Abers and Morlaix bay in the far west, despite an outbreak in the 1970s in two estuaries, Aber Wrac'h and Aber Benoît, of a mysterious parasitic disease which spread around the coasts of the promontory as far as Brest and Arcachon to the south and the Bay of Brieuc in the north. Aber Disease, as it became known, severely affected Brittany's oyster trade for several years but now appears to have been brought under control. However, foreign and cheaper *creuses*—hollow oysters imported from Portugal and now from as far away as Japan and British Columbia—are in greater demand than ever.

Drink

One hesitates to head this section 'Wine' as Brittany has none to speak of. The nearest thing to a Brittany wine is Muscadet, which goes well with most kinds of fish and especially oysters and the best of which come from the vineyards south-east from Nantes, no longer officially a Breton city. The lesser VDQS wine Gros Plant, rather dry and acidic to some tastes but quite often fruity and refreshing, is made from a grape of the same name which grows in that area too. Muscadet and Gros Plant are the two wines that are most widely available in Brittany and for those who would like to make a detour to taste and buy, details of the vineyards and their locations are given in the companion volume in this series, *The Loire Valley* by Arthur and Barbara Eperon.

Some wine is produced on the Rhuys peninsula but doesn't travel well. It even has a mixed reputation locally, where they will tell you that to drink it requires four men and a wall: 'one to pour it, one to drink it, two to hold him and the wall to stop him from falling backwards'. Liqueurs and spirits are distilled in Brittany: a heavy mead or *hydromel* which is usually labelled 'Chouchenn', *lambic*, a cider liqueur, or the distinctive sweet liqueur made from strawberries grown at Plougastel. The distillery at Lannion which produces the latter even manufactures a Breton whisky.

Most local people prefer cider: '*Au Breton gourmand ce qui pétille est bon*'. On the whole, Norman cider is better than Breton, which equates with the 'scrumpy' of the West of England, save for that produced around Fouesnant, Clohars, Pleudihen and Beg-Meil, which is superior. Much of it comes from small producers in a network of *fabrication artisanale*. If offered cider from a barrel or a bottle at a *pardon* it is wise to choose the bottled stuff as the former is calculated to have a similar effect to Rhuys wine.

Part One:
Haute Bretagne

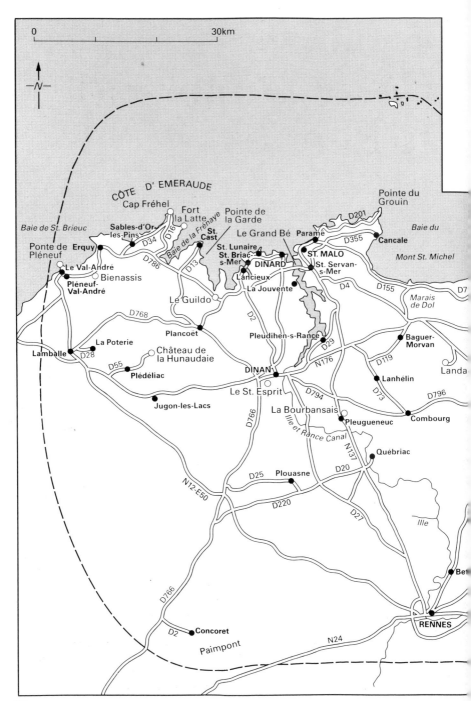

4
Côte D'Émeraude to Rennes

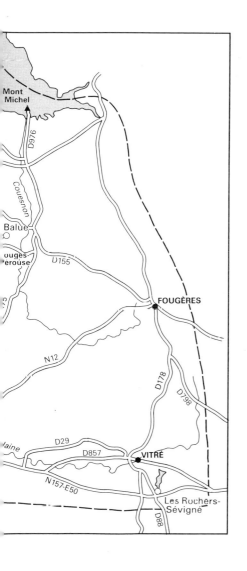

St. Malo to Dinan and Beyond

The people of **St. Malo** have a saying 'Malouin d'abord, Breton peut-être, français s'il en reste' which means they are malouins first, Breton next and French if there is anything left. It sums up the frontier mentality and the separateness of the whole of Brittany. Approaching from the sea aboard a Brittany Ferries vessel, the cannon on the ramparts of the old town within the walls, St. Malo Intra-Muros, dominated by the towers of the château at the landward side, reinforce this impression of insularity. Here from a secure anchorage at the mouth of the River Rance, the malouin corsairs challenged the maritime powers of the world. Inland from the English Channel to the Atlantic, across the neck of the Breton peninsula, there is a frontier of citadels against the rest of France.

Strolling on the ramparts of St. Malo Intra-Muros, gazing out to sea with the statues of its famous sons, across the estuary to Dinard, or inwards on to the slate roofs and into the upper windows of the granite houses, it is difficult to believe that it is a superb fake.

29

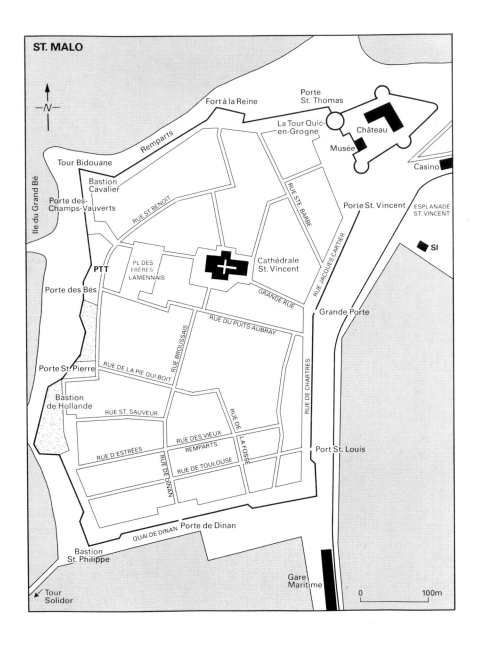

The Corsairs of St. Malo

If it seems strange that a city should boast of its pirates—St. Malo calls itself the Cité Corsaire—rather than its sons such as Jacques Cartier and Mahe La Bourdonnais who discovered new lands, or Chateaubriand, its greatest writer, it is necessary to point out that they were not really pirates at all. They did not hoist the Jolly Roger but were obliged to show their proper colours before opening fire. The corsairs were licensed by the Crown and issued with letters of marque signed by the King entitling them to board and seize a variety of vessels, not merely those of a hostile power but also those who simply refused to stop or to disclose their nationality. The prize had to be sailed back to France and handed over to the navy for division of the spoils. The Crown took a ten per cent cut and of the rest, a third went to the crew and two-thirds to the *armateur* or shipowner.

Little wonder that the *armateurs* of St. Malo grew rich on the proceeds. The remnants of their mansions can be seen in the countryside beyond the ramparts of the city and the statues of the two most famous corsairs, René Duguay-Trouin and Robert Surcouf, survey the scene from within the walls.

As a boy, Duguay-Trouin was intended for the priesthood but instead was schooled by an inveterate gambler and womaniser before going to sea and becoming a corsair commander before he was 20. The St. Malo of his day was full of brothels and gambling houses. Between 1692 to 1712 he captured or sank 85 ships flying the English flag, including 10 men-of-war, plus nine fighting ships and 94 merchantmen of other nationalities. For a year he was held prisoner at Plymouth until he acquired a longboat fitted with a sail, six oars, six muskets and six sabres, biscuits, beer, a compass 'and other necessary provisions' and made his escape. The culmination of his brief but spectacular career was his capture of Rio de Janeiro from the Portuguese in 1711. The following year he returned to France in poor health, hardly ever venturing to sea again. He died in 1736 at the age of 63.

Robert Surcouf was born nearly 50 years later to a wealthy *armateur* family and ran away from school in Dinan. Like Duguay-Trouin he achieved command of his own vessel at 20 and became the scourge of the East India Company's ships in the Indian Ocean. In 1800 he captured the *Kent*, a ship of 1,200 tons with 38 guns, carrying a complement of 437 and a number of passengers, including several women, after ferocious hand-to-hand fighting with cutlass and shot. Surcouf did so well out of swashbuckling that he was able to retire to St. Malo on the proceeds at the age of 36. He died in 1827.

Not every *malouin* mariner was a pirate, however. Porcon de la Bardinais was captain of a St. Malo frigate sent to protect French merchantmen against the Barbary Coast pirates during the reign of Louis XIV. During one encounter he was captured and taken to the Bey of Algiers, who, instead of sending him into slavery at the oars of the galleys, which was the usual fate of prisoners, despatched him to France with peace proposals for the king. The condition was imposed that Porcon would return to captivity if the proposals were rejected. They were and the captain duly returned to Algiers with the answer, which so angered the Bey that he had de la Bardinais blown to pieces at the mouth of a cannon!

The city was all but gutted during a two-week siege in August 1944 when General George Patton's 8th Army Corps and the German defenders were dug in at opposite sides of the old town hurling shells, bombs and rockets at each other, with further bombardment from ships out at sea and air raids. St. Malo burned and when the German commander eventually surrendered little of it was left, apart from the stoutest sections of walls and buildings. However, it has been rebuilt with admirable faithfulness to its 12th- to 18th-century origins, with 20th-century advantages of efficient drains and electric power. You have to search for the pockmarks of shot and shrapnel in façades before deciding whether they are genuine or 'repro'. Only a scrawl of graffiti on some of the ancient cannons spoils the medieval illusion.

It takes about 30 minutes to walk the walls. At intervals there are bastions and fortified towers such as the Quic-en-Groigne which houses a display of the corsairs and their swashbuckling deeds. The Musée d'Histoire near the St. Vincent gateway presents a less melodramatic but none the less fascinating display of St. Malo's past from the explorations of Jacques Cartier which opened up Canada to the French to portraits of Chateaubriand and the great priest-philosopher Lamennais, the son of a St. Malo shipowner. The museum's collection of photographs from World War II shows just how great was the devastation of the city that has since risen from the ashes. St. Malo

The walled town of St. Malo was completely rebuilt after World War II

33

The interior of St. Malo Cathedral is bathed in light through its modern stained glass

today is a resort as much as a port. There's a Casino and the Tourist Office on the Esplanade St. Vincent is well supplied with maps and brochures.

The Cathedral of St. Vincent is distinguished by its modern stained glass, casting a kaleidoscope of colours on to the ancient pillars inside and bathing the side altar in ethereal light. Access to a sandy beach with its own seawater swimming pool and diving tower at the foot of the ramparts is by a gate in the walls. Just offshore is the island of **Le Grand Bé** where Chateaubriand is buried. It can be reached on foot across a causeway at low tide. On the landward side of St. Malo Intra-Muros, within easy walking distance, is the Gare Maritime with its ample car parks

and comfortable waiting rooms. Cross-Channel ferries ply between here and Portsmouth and there are car ferry and fast hydrofoil services to the Channel Islands.

Paramé to the east is almost literally overshadowed by its famous neighbour yet it is well supplied with comfortable hotels and pensions covering the whole price range and should not be overlooked when St. Malo is bursting at the seams in summer. To the south of the crowded St. Malo *bassins* is the town of **St. Servan-sur-Mer** which has a sheltered, sandy beach and swimming pool with a chute as well as a diving board, numerous shops, hotels, restaurants and ships' chandleries, an attractive church and a handsome town hall. A walk around the Corniche d'Aleth beyond the Anse des Sablons and past the 18th-century City Fort brings you to the site where the Welsh saint St. Malo landed in the 6th century, the original settlement of the Gauls and later the Romans. St. Malo Intra-Muros wasn't built until the middle of the 12th century. Continuing around the Aleth promontory, the triple towers of the Tour Solidor built in 1382 after the Wars of Succession by Duke Jean IV to keep the unhelpful *malouins* in their place rise above two flanking harbours. The tower houses a museum of the Cape Horners and offers excellent views of the Rance Estuary in one direction and the battlements of St. Malo to the north.

It is possible to take a 10-minute ferry trip across the estuary to the resort of **Dinard**, which was 'discovered' by the Victorian middle classes from England and retains a certain period charm. The main road there (D168) has to cross the Rance over the great dam just south of St. Servan. When it was opened in 1967 it was the first in the world to use tidal power to generate electricity. It is an impressive sight when the sluice gates are opened, allowing the pent-up waters to rush out, and quite alarming for leisure sailors who are new to it—levels in the river above the dam can fall by a metre in as little as ten minutes.

Going upriver on one of the regular Vedettes Blanches trips, you rise rapidly with the water in the lock and sail out into what appears as a broad lake behind the dam before high wooded banks close in. It takes two and a half hours to travel the 22km to Dinan from St. Malo or Dinard compared to 30 minutes by road, but it is a much more enjoyable journey scenically, as all along the valley are little jetties, boatyards, mills turned by the tides, humble cottages as well as *malouinières*, the lavishly decorated mansions of the shipowners of St. Malo, some of them now in a state of disrepair with crumbling walls and derelict summer houses. Fortifications are a reminder that this was always a strategic river, pillaged by the Vikings, attacked by the English, and defended by the tough seafarers of St. Malo. But the history of settlement in this area goes back to before the Middle Ages. The best of the few surviving Gallo-Roman remains in Brittany are to be found here. The **Temple of Mars** stands in open country south-east of **Corseul** and at **Taden**, where the old Roman road crossed the river on its way from Corseul to Dol, there are the ruins of a large Gallo-Roman villa. At nearby **St. Solen** the standing stone of La Tiemblaye, covered with neolithic signs, is a reminder of an even earlier civilisation. According to legend, the *jetins*, mis-chievous water elves, inhabited the river banks long before the Irish saints, St. Suliac and St. Buc, arrived from over the water in their stone boats.

By the time it reaches **Dinan**, the Rance has crossed the departmental border from Ille-et-Vilaine into Côtes-du-Nord and is little wider than a canal. It continues its southward journey, crossing back into Ille-et-Vilaine sometimes as a canal jointly with the River Ille until they meet up with the Vilaine at Rennes 85km away to form a waterway to the southern coast of Brittany. At Dinan a path zig-zags upwards from the quay, once busy with commercial shipping but now used mostly by pleasure craft, to the ramparts of Dinan on the rocky crag above and the delightful Jardin Anglais with its wide views of the river

The triple towers of the 14th-century Tour Solidor dominate St. Servan

valley, the 40m-high viaduct of Vieux-Pont (built in 1852) and the surrounding countryside. In this lovely public garden, amidst the trees and early flowering shrubs, is the 12th-century basilica of St. Sauveur, wherein lies the heart of the knight Bertrand du Guesclin, who spent a life in chivalrous combat with the English. The stained glass windows depict the martyrdom of the patron saints of various trades and there is a monument to St. Roch, credited with having lifted a plague from Dinan in the 16th century.

Du Guesclin (see Box) was born near Dinan and married a Dinan draper's daughter. The spacious place du Guesclin contains his statue mounted on horseback among rank upon rank of parked cars. Next to it is Dinan's other main square, place du Champ Clos. A market is held on this medieval fairground on Thursday mornings.

Like most of these Breton fortified towns, Dinan is in a marvellous state of preservation, effortlessly conjuring up its own vivid history for us with its château, built into the south west walls of the town between 1382 and 1387, its quaint streets and alleyways. Three distinct kinds of half-timbered houses can be seen: à porche, where the upper storeys are supported by pillars of granite or wood, forming arcades over the pavement; 15th-century houses with stepped-out upper storeys; casement houses with big windows made by ships' carpenters to resemble the stern galleries of galleons. If you come by car it is best to leave it in one of the squares or car parks around the walls (if you are lucky enough to find a vacant space)

The River Rance at Dinan is a waterway for pleasure boats

Bertrand du Guesclin (1320–1380)

Bertrand du Guesclin was born at La Motte Broom castle just north of Dinan and the battlemented town contains various memorials to the man who became Constable of France. In the tree-shaded place du Champ-Clos, a statue of the knight mounted on a horse marks the very ground on which he left Sir Thomas Canterbury dead after accepting his challenge to a duel. This medieval feat of arms took place in 1359 during the War of Succession when du Guesclin held Dinan against the English forces led by the Duke of Lancaster. The war ended with the Battle of Auray in 1364 with the defeat of Charles of Blois, who was killed.

During the battle, du Guesclin was unhorsed but an English knight, John Chandos, came to his rescue and persuaded him to give up his sword, remarking 'This day cannot be yours but there will, *certes*, be another!' Prophetic words, for although England backed the successful de Montforts in their contention for the Duchy of Brittany, France benefited from du Guesclin's subsequent services. Released from captivity for a ransom of 100,000 crowns, he went on to serve the new King of France, Charles the Wise, with an army known as the *Grandes Compagnies* in battle after battle, becoming Constable (Commander-in-Chief). Throughout his military career he directed his efforts to driving the English out of France and he died (of a fever) while besieging them at Châteauneuf-de-Randon in the Massif Central.

To Breton separatists France is now, as then, another country. That is why in his homeland, du Guesclin was vilified as a traitor for having marched against Duke Jean on the orders of the king. As recently as 1946 his statue at Rennes was blown up by Breton nationalists.

and take a leisurely stroll through the narrow streets, fine squares and gardens, and follow the ramparts around the city. Nearly 4km long and laid out in the 13th century, these walls are almost completely intact apart from a gap left by the demolition of the Porte de Brest in 1880. The streets and squares within the walls evoke the names of medieval guilds: place des Cordeliers, place des Merciers, rue de la Lainerie. Rue de Jerzual is the street of artists, sculptors and craftsmen, and don't miss the street of the clockmakers, rue d'Horloge, graced with a curious 15th-century clock tower and the 16th-century House of the Effigy.

The Syndicat d'Initiative is here, too, in the Keratry mansion built in 1559. They will provide you with an excellent little brochure in English listing all the sights but will charge you for it. Dinan is very much a tourist town. Chateaubriand went to school here and the Duchess Anne took shelter from her enemies in the Château in 1507. There is a Promenade de la Duchesse Anne along the town walls overlooking the Rance and the Donjon de la Duchesse Anne inside the castle, which houses the local museum. The keep is some 40m high, of an unusual oval shape with distinctive machicolation.

In high summer it can be a relief to

escape from the hot crowded streets through the twin-arched Renaissance entry on the Grand Rue into the cool, austere interior of St. Malo Church. Begun in 1490 and finished in the 19th century, the church is built around two rows of columns. It has an English Romantic organ with polychrome pipes, listed as an historical monument. There are good average hotels and restaurants within the town walls, of which the d'Avaugour in the place du Champ Clos is the best despite the amount of traffic outside.

A favourite walk of the Dinannais is down rue de Jerzual and across the old bridge, turning right to follow the towpath upstream, under the viaduct, across the meadows to **Léhon**. It is a fascinating little place with ruins of a castle and an abbey founded c.850 by six Breton monks who found favour with Nominoë, first King of Brittany, by adopting St. Magloire, Bishop of Dol, as their patron saint. Among the effigies in the nave of the restored 5th-century abbey church with magnificent cloisters is that of du Guesclin's wife, the beautiful and intelligent Typhaine, surprisingly clad in full armour. West of Léhon at **Le St.-Esprit** is a wayside cross erected in 1359 by John of Gaunt when he had Dinan under siege. Nearly 8m high, it supports two statues, God holding up Christ and the crowning of the Virgin Mary.

The countryside south of here to **Hédé**, where there is a ruined castle and a flight of eleven locks on the Ille et Rance Canal, is delightfully unspoiled. The main route is the D794 then the N137 but more interesting minor roads cross and recross the canal. The **Château de la Bourbansais** outside **Pleugueneuc** has classical gardens and a wildlife park

with zebras and lions. The village of **Tinténiac** is worth visiting for its abundance of flowers, growing everywhere, and is a favoured port of call for boating people. The castle at **Combourg**, eastward on the D/94, is altogether more forbidding but Chateaubriand was brought up there, and anyone who has read his memoirs of his sad childhood ('It is in the woods of Combourg that I became what I am') will want to see it. It was originally owned by the du Guesclin family in the 11th century. The 14th-century duel of Bertrand and the English knight is re-enacted in full armour on horseback on various summer evenings at the Abbey of **Le Tronchet**, 10km north-west of Combourg on the D73) amidst beautiful lakes and forests, (the setting also for one of the best of Brittany's golf courses.

Dinard to St. Brieuc Bay

Opposite St. Malo across the Rance lies **Dinard**, variously known as 'the Pearl of the Côte d'Émeraude' or the 'Nice of the North'. It is a stylish place with more than a touch of the Belle Époque about it and there is no better introduction to its charms on a fine morning than to stroll along the Promenade du Clair de Lune from the main Plage du l'Écluse around the Pointe du Moulinet to the Plage du Prieuré. Dinard claims the highest tides in the world and its movements are spectacular. The smell of the

Combourg town and the château where the great writer Chateaubriand was born

sea mingles with the scents of the flowers in the well-tended gardens along the promenade, the gun on the Yacht Club terrace booms for the start of a race, echoing out towards the offshore islands and the citadel of St. Malo brooding on the horizon. In a flower-filled grotto, a statue of the Virgin Mary invites us to 'pray for our fishermen'. Until it was 'discovered' by the *bourgeoisie* in the middle of the last century Dinard *was* simply a fishing village. An American built a mock château there and the middle classes from Victorian England followed in droves, in search of something rather more exciting than Bournemouth.

But gentility ruled on the other side of the Channel, too. In a book called *Breton Folk* published in 1880 Henry Blackburn writes: 'At Dinard you play at croquet on the sand; at St. Briac you scramble over granite rocks, and fish in the pools under their shadows; at St. Jacut you wander over the sands with a shrimp net and in the evenings help the nuns to draw water from the well.'

The Casino is still thriving, but in a renovated and modernised Palais d'Ém-eraude in the boulevard du Président Wilson overlooking the Plage de l'Écluse and Cézembre island. A bar, tea room, restaurant and nightclub are part of the facilities. Roulette, boule and 'Le Black-Jack' are all played. On the beaches volleyball is popular with the young while their elders play boules. Dinard has three fine sandy beaches. St. Énogat, where the resort began, is a favourite of young families with the children queuing up for their Mickey Club plastic bags at the end of the day's supervised romps. The semi-circular Plage de l'Écluse looks like the perfect seaside picture postcard with its bright

flags and serried ranks of beach tents with a seawater swimming pool at one end. There is another open air seawater pool at the beginning of the Plage du Prieuré, which has a 4-star camping site only 200m from it.

All these beaches are safe for bathing, with instructors available for swimming lessons and physical training. There are organised beach games for the children. The climate benefits from the Gulf Stream with average temperatures ranging from 15°C to 18°C in May and September to 20°C in July and August. Mimosa and camellia are in flower in February and there are even a few palm trees and eucalyptus. However, if the weather is unkind, an indoor heated seawater swimming pool of Olympic dimensions (50 x 18m) in the town centre is open all year except January. Dinard Tennis Club, also in the town centre, has 11 courts (including one indoors) open year round. There are facilities for riding and fishing. An 18-hole golf course is available by the sea at St. Briac, 7.5km out of town, where numerous championships are held. Yacht races are held almost every day during summer and there are several approved sailing and windsurfing schools.

However, Dinard isn't just for the outdoor, sporty type. The Bridge Club, open every afternoon, arranges tournaments twice a week and holds international competitions. The Musée Historique in the Villa Eugénie at 12 rue des Français Libres near the Plage du Prieuré gives video presentations on prehistory and archaeology and holds expositions of local history such as the Belle Époque villas of the town. It is open 2-6pm. Dinard plays host during August to the Académie Internationale

François René Chateaubriand (1768–1848)

Monuments to St. Malo's most famous son—writer, statesman and exile—are numerous in Brittany. Beaufil's statue of him dominates the ramparts of the corsair city. His burial place on the nearby island of Le Grand Bé is marked by a granite cross facing the sea. Combourg Castle, his birthplace and the family seat 30 km south-east of the town, is today open to visitors. He grew up there and went to school in the equally handsome town of Dinan upriver on the Rance.

As a young man, René was involved in soldiering and diplomacy, both activities considered suitable for someone of his background. But returning from a visit to America after the Revolution in France, he was sent into exile for five years.

It was during this period that his writing talent emerged in *Atala* and the autobiographical *René* which was to form part of his *Le Génie du Christianisme* published in 1802. He continued writing into old age, returning to diplomacy after helping Louis XVIII to gain the throne in 1814 and holding various posts. His best known work *Mémoires d'Outre-Tombe* appeared in 1849, the year following his death.

A contemporary of Wordsworth, he was one of the earliest Romantics, but he died a frustrated man, having failed to achieve many of his cherished ambitions and having had a sad childhood followed by an unhappy marriage.

de Musique and the Académie Internationale de Danse and from June to September the *spectacle d'ambiance* bathes the 'moonlight Promenade' in lights and the music of Bach, Beethoven, Mozart, Debussy and other classical composers. There are firework displays in July and August and market days on Tuesdays, Thursdays and Saturdays. Dinard *is* a lively town and the busy Tourist Office at 2 boulevard Féart will supply free of charge a mountain of brochures, maps and lists of accommodation, which ranges from smart hotels with sea views to bed and breakfast, self-catering, camping sites, youth hostels to *gîtes* in the surrounding countryside. Dinard makes a good base for exploring the Côte d'Émeraude or inland. Its rail and road connections are good and the airport, 5km out of town, has regular flights from Paris and London (via Jersey). Jersey, only 20 minutes flying time away, is a day trip destination. Excursions can be made by coach to Dinan, Cap Fréhel, Mont St. Michel or further afield, or by boat to St. Malo, Chausey Island, Cap Fréhel, across the Bay of Mont St. Michel or not least in the Bay of Dinard and the River Rance as far as Dinan. 'Gourmet cruises' are held aboard the bateau-restaurant *Châteaubriand*.

Just west of Dinard on the D786, **St. Lunaire** has two beaches, the main one sheltered by pines and the larger one, called Longchamps. There is 3-star

camping here in a green setting 300m from the sands. **St. Briac-sur-Mer**, a little further around the headland, is a picturesque spot with lovely bays, sandy beaches and small islands offshore. Its 18-hole golf course, the second oldest in France, serves Dinard. In windy weather the cliff top holes can be difficult. On the second Sunday of August St. Briac celebrates its Fêtes des Mouettes (seagulls) with hundreds of bagpipers and dancers from all over Brittany in a Défilé en Ville, a procession through the town. This is followed by a festival of folk dancing and a Fest-Noz, night festival.

The Fremur River flows into the sea at St. Briac, marking the border between the *départements* of Ille-et-Vilaine and Côtes-du-Nord. The first resort we come to in the latter is **Lancieux** standing on a large inlet of the sea with an excellent beach sheltered by rocks at each end. Tennis courts provide an energetic alternative to snoozing on the sand between dips in the sea. After **Ploubalay**, the D786 runs through a pleasant coastal landscape, where it crosses the estuary of the Arguenon, which means 'White River'; the ruined castle of **Le Guildo** can be glimpsed from the bridge.

A memorial to the defeat of the British invaders in the Battle of St. Cast stands on the cliffs high on the peninsula of **St. Cast-le-Guildo**, which these days offers just about everything needed for a restful family holiday with seven well-screened beaches and little harbours for fishing and pleasure boats. There are 23 hotels, over 2,000 flats to

The promenade at Dinard is the scene of summer concerts

let and eight camping sites from basic to classy. Facilities for indoor swimming, tennis, golf, sailing and riding are laid on. Dinard and St. Malo are a bus or a boat ride away. Inland, pinewoods and ponds alternate with orchards and fields. Adjoining St. Cast are **Pen Guen**, its long beach fringed by the dunes and pines, and **La Garde**, at the southern end of the bay beside the best of the beaches. Footpaths wind along the cliff-top from St. Cast harbour to the far end of La Frênaye bay past the beaches of La Mare and La Pissotte (ramble path GR34).

On the western side of the Baie de la Frênaye another peninsula is dominated by the red and black cliffs of **Cap Fréhel** rising 70m from the surf crashing on the rocks below. Gulls, terns and cormorants swoop from seemingly impossible perches in the sheer natural wall. From the D786 beyond **Matig-**

Vauban's impregnable Fort la Latte has two drawbridges

non, route D16 climbs up to the lighthouse perched on the summit standing guard over the shoals and reefs of the Côte d'Émeraude. Its light can be seen 110km out to sea. This coast, which looks so enchanting in fine weather, can be treacherous in storms or fogs when visibility is down to a few metres. This lighthouse is one of several in Brittany that are open to visitors by appointment with the keepers (see details in Practical Information at the end of this book). There is an unpretentious inn with splendid views, the Relais de Fréhel.

Across the Bay of Sévignés from Cap Fréhel, **Fort La Latte** stands guard on the point opposite St. Cast. The corsairs who built it in the Middle Ages used the cliffs to strengthen its bulwarks on the seaward side (there is, incidentally, a nice secluded bathing beach at the foot of it). Inland, the fort has two drawbridges over a double crevasse. The original fortifications were improved upon in the 17th century by Sebastien Vauban, Louis XIV's military architect who also worked on the citadel town of St. Malo. Gargantua's Finger, a mysterious standing stone, broods over the approach to the forbidding battlements. Fort La Latte has a curious oven, installed in 1795, for heating cannon balls before they were fired at enemy ships.

Both Fort La Latte and Cap Fréhel provide magnificent vantage points for views up and down the Côte d'Émeraude. From the lighthouse the scenic D34A and D34 roads wind down towards Sables-d'Or-les-Pins and beside it is a path for ramblers (GR34). The views of land and seascape are impressive, whichever mode of transport you choose. On the way is the village of

Vieux Bourg de Pléhérel, perched on the cliff top with pine-fringed sands below. The hotel Plage et Fréhel offers comfortable rooms at a moderate price and the cheaper menu in the restaurant is good. **Les Sables-d'Or-les-Pins** is as charming as its name suggests, with a variety of medium price hotels and restaurants to choose from, a 9-hole golf course and a splendid stretch of beach besides the dunes and pines. **Erquy-Plages**, a little further along the D786, lives up to its name, too, with no fewer than seven beaches of white sand cleaned twice a day by the powerful tides that scour the whole of the Côte d'Émeraude. There is not much organised entertainment here but that is part of its charm. Near Erquy is Bienassis Castle dating from the 15th and 16th centuries with a moat, ramparts and formal gardens.

For 9km south-west of Erquy the gleaming sands stretch all the way to **Pléneuf-Val-André** together with new vistas of the great Bay of St. Brieuc. Le Val-André is a graceful resort with a well-tended promenade and gardens and is large enough to boast a casino, a concert hall and 17 tennis courts. It is worth visiting for its restaurants alone, especially the modestly priced Le Biniou (Breton for bagpipe) or the more expensive Cotriade, which has a Michelin star. The rocky Pointe de Pléneuf guards the northern tip of the 2km sandy beach.

Seventeen kilometres inland from Pléneuf-Val-André on the D791, the ancient town of **Lamballe** is renowned for its stud farm, one of the largest in France, which produces Trait Breton draught horses as well as French and Anglo-Arab saddle horses. Guided tours are held from 10 July to 15 September. It houses part of the French National Stud. Alas, it seems that some of its stock is used to breed flesh for the horse butchers who still flourish in France beneath the traditional sign of a golden horse's head.

Lamballe's other main claim to fame is the princess, lady-in-waiting to Marie-Antoinette, who took her name from the town. Unfortunately, the Princesse de Lamballe lost her head when she was carried to the guillotine by the revolutionaries in 1792. Lamballe's history is visible, in its buildings such as the Collégiale Notre-Dame dating from the 16th and 17th centuries and the 15th-century Executioner's House. It is linked by motorway to St. Brieuc, capital of the Côtes-du-Nord, 21km to the west, and the N176 is the main highway back to Dinan, 40km east, and thence to Dinard or St. Malo. Within 20km is **Jugon-les-Lacs** with gracious period houses and a 100-hectare lake for fishing, sailing or just swimming, the Cistercian abbey of Boquen founded in the 12th century and the 'site de Croquelien' where the granite boulders are depicted as being the fairy Margot's cot, chair or platter.

St. Malo to Le Mont St. Michel

The journey eastwards along the Côte d'Émeraude from St. Malo starts quietly enough through **Paramé** and **Rochebonne** which are virtually suburbs of the walled city, past villa-like hotels amid pines facing the sandy beach. There is more of the same at **Rothéneuf** (and very nice, too). Beyond there the

Fine lamb comes from the marshes of Dol

Pointe du Grouin provides a *counter-point* to Cap Fréhel and serves as a dramatic introduction to the vast Bay of Mont St. Michel. To see it to best effect, follow the corniche route D201, or, even better, the footpath GR34, although if you are in a hurry there are different highways to Cancale or Dol. Twenty-five years ago only cart tracks led to the shore around here and even

today it is possible to experience peaceful isolation even at the height of summer. The coast road and path lead past almost deserted coves and quiet stretches of tide-washed sands.

Just outside Cancale on the D355 from St. Malo is the birthplace of Jeanne Jugon, who founded the Little Sisters of the Poor. The daughter of a local fisherman, she was born in 1792 and as soon as she was old enough was sent into domestic service at St. Servan. A legacy of 400 francs on the death of her mistress gave her the opportunity to found the charitable order which spread around the world.

At the very tip of the **Pointe du Grouin**, the finger of land which points out to sea towards the Channel Isles, is the **Île des Landes** nature reserve, where binoculars are a must. Just out to sea, perched on a rock, is the lighthouse of **La Pierre de Herpin**, not, like its partner on the far side of St. Malo, accessible to visitors. There is another quiet, inexpensive hotel here, the Pointe du Grouin.

Cancale, 4.5km south on the D201 passing close to the fine beaches of Port-Mer and Port-Briac, is a little port devoted to oysters. Its quays and jetties and the streets running down to the lower port are lined with restaurants, bars and stalls where the bivalves are sold, from smart establishments with prices to match up to 170F and above to fishwives who will sell you a dozen for a modest franc note. Away from the Port de la Houle, in rue Duguesclin, Michelin-starred de Bricourt represents the pinnacle of oyster *dégustation* together with roast oyster and *pré-salé* lamb from the nearby marshes, but it is very expensive and nearly always booked out. Le Cancalais or Ty Breiz on the quai Gambetta or Phare beside the port (which also has inexpensive rooms to let) are just some of the alternatives, while numerous bars provide a plateful of oysters and a half-bottle of Muscadet or Gros Plant to wash them down at a moderate price.

From the Pointe du Hock or the jetty, the oyster beds in the Bay of Mont St.

Michel can be viewed. When the tide is at its lowest every two weeks or so, the *chalands* or motorised platforms putter two or three kilometres out in a small fleet to tend the growing crop. The biggest oysters (*pieds de cheval*) are grown directly on the seabed just offshore. Cultivating oysters is back-breaking work extended over three or four years. The final stage is at the *parcs* near the jetty where the fully grown oysters are cleansed of mud and internal impurities.

The red-sailed oyster smacks or *bisquines*, in one of which the composer Claude Debussy sailed when he visited Cancale and experienced the storm which inspired him to write *La Mer*, no longer exist, alas, other than in paintings or old photographs and one 17m craft restored by the Association la Bisquine Cancalaise—trips can be taken in this vessel (tel.99.89.88.87). A much more modern kind of boat, equipped with wheels for running on the mudflats at low tide, is the *Sirène de la Baie*. It carries 150 passengers on cruises around the Bay of Mont St. Michel, visiting the offshore beds where oysters and mussels are cultivated and serving them, or a gourmet menu, on board. The cruises start from **Le Vivier-sur-Mer**, a 15km drive from Cancale by the D76 and the D155 crossing hectare after hectare of reclaimed shore where there are few good beaches and the sea often out of sight beyond seemingly endless mudflats. The rows of poles (*bouchots*) on which mussels are cultivated extend to a total of 210km, a few kilometres offshore from Le Vivier, which in the past three decades has grown to become the centre of *mytiliculture* in France, producing between 10,000 and 12,000 tonnes per year.

Jacques Cartier (1491–1557)

It is an oddity of history that the Breton who discovered Canada and claimed it for the French is so little honoured in his native country. In St. Malo, the port from which he sailed in 1534 in search of a Northwest passage and gold, he is overshadowed by the corsairs. The only substantial monument to Jacques Cartier is the Limoelou manor house at **Rothéneuf**, a little way to the east of St. Malo, which was his home when he wasn't away adventuring on the high seas. Somewhat belatedly, this has been restored and furnished in period style to tell the story of Cartier's daily life and travels. He was well into middle age when he embarked on his epic journey to the shores of Newfoundland. On his second voyage two years later he sailed up the St. Lawrence River and renamed the Indian village of Hochelaga, Montreal (Mount royal). In 1541 and 1543 he made further voyages to consolidate French Canada. The loss of these colonies to the English in the 18th century when Louis XV was on the throne seems to have obliterated Cartier's niche in the hall of fame alongside the great navigators such as Columbus and Cook. His manor house dating from the 15th and 16th centuries is open to visitors from the beginning of June to the end of September and is well worth visiting.

Turning inland on the D155, a 120m-high granite outcrop rears out of the alluvial plain like a gigantic standing stone, the only hill in sight. This is **Mont Dol**, which was an island when the sea reached inland to Dol-de-Bretagne. Before that, in prehistoric times, it was a mountain in a wood and the fossilised remains of mammoths and dinosaurs have been found here. In legend, it is the place where St. Michael duelled with the Devil and marks in the rocks are said to be Satan's claw marks as he fell and Michael's footprint as he bounded off towards his stronghold at Mont St. Michel across the bay. Identification of the marks is left very much to the individual visitor. Whatever the accuracy of the story, Mont Dol was a holy place of the Celts and hermits sought its solitude. There is a rather sad chapel with a tower on its summit, worth visiting only for its views of the surrounding marshes and the sea.

Dol-de-Bretagne is a remarkable place, a quiet backwater dreaming of 1,300 years of ecclesiastical prominence, of kings and bishops and saints with supernatural powers. The main street is lined with medieval houses forming arcades and the tree-shaded promenade behind the cathedral looks across the plain that once was open sea to the strange hump of Mont Dol.

A mere 13km to the southeast on byroads off the D155 to Antrain is a lovely Renaissance castle in a setting of woods and small lakes. The **Château de Landal** is not open to visitors but its courtyard, ramparts and grounds are. In total contrast, the countryside between Dol and Mont St. Michel is mostly salt marsh and polder, reminiscent of Holland, criss-crossed by canals, its windswept pastures grazed by sheep and lambs which provide the *pré-salé* meat which is one of the delights of Breton cuisine. What few trees grow here are mostly hung with ivy. In the distance, on the far shore of the Couesnon River, the spires and battlements of an island fortress prick the flat horizon like a mirage.

Le Mont St. Michel, strictly speaking, is not in Brittany but in Normandy. The violent sweep of the tides in and out of the great bay of Mont St. Michel has in the past changed the course of the Couesnon, which marks the frontier between the two historic Duchies. The 8th-century fortified abbey perched on its granite platform above the sea and the polders is worth a detour on the D976 from Pontorson to see it at close quarters. There is no more famous—or popular—sight in France outside Paris.

Approaching it from the car park on the causeway involves climbing steep flights of stone steps and once inside the walls the climb continues until the visitor reaches the Romanesque and Gothic abbey at the pinnacle. At this point the crowds have thinned dramatically. There are garden walks, panoramic views and a museum.

When the tide is out, the sea is 15km from Mont St. Michel but it comes in at great speed, surrounding the citadel apart from the causeway which links it to the shore. It is as well to bear this in mind if you take a walk, as many do, on the expanse of muddy sand stretching away from the ramparts at low tide. The whole area is a magnet for ramblers. A waymarked trail (GR34) cuts across the polders from Mont St. Michel and continues westward along the coast around the Pointe de Grouin. GR22 is the walkers' coastal route eastwards into Normandy and southwards GR39 follows the Couesnon towards Pontorson and Antrain.

Le Mont St. Michel to Rennes

Having bypassed Mont St. Michel, route N175 rushes headlong southwards from Pontorson towards Rennes. But it's worth making a detour on the D155 from Antrain to take a look at Brittany's citadel frontier; not that there *is* a real frontier dividing Brittany and France but, as at Mont St. Michel, it feels like one, the legacy of the warring fiefdoms of the past. Nowhere is this better illustrated than at **Fougères**, a town built around a massive château which stands, unusually, in a green valley rather than atop a hill. It uses the Nançon River, by which it stands, to fill a great moat. The first castle was built

The massive château of Fougères is part of Brittany's inland 'citadel frontier'

51

on this site almost a thousand years ago and was razed by the English Plantaganet Henry II in the 12th century when he tried to seize the Duchy. Its unrepentant owner, Raoul II, rebuilt it and parts of his fortifications survive with the additions of the 13th and 14th centuries. Fougères was repeatedly under siege and changing hands during the Hundred Years' War.

A pleasant way to approach the castle is on foot from the most helpful Syndicat d'Initiative office in place Aristide-Briand, down the rue Nationale, an attractive stone-paved and traffic-free thoroughfare lined with outdoor cafés and fountains, to the Church of St. Léonard. Beyond, shady paths wind down a steep hill on which public gardens are terraced (place aux Arbres). The view through the leaves includes the château, the Gothic church of St. Sulpice beside it and the surrounding countryside.

The castle, which is sometimes used as an open-air theatre, is open to visitors and contains a Shoe Museum, with exhibits from all over the world and as far back as the 16th century. Fougères is a shoe-manufacturing town, selling its wares in Paris, as well as being a town of art and history. At 51 rue Nationale is a museum devoted entirely to Emmanuel de la Villeon (1858-1944) one of the last great Impressionist painters, who was born at Fougères.

After walking the ramparts and climbing the Melusine tower for another view of the town, the rue de la Pinterie climbs the hill from the château back to the *haute ville*. Fougères is in

Le Mont St. Michel, no longer in Brittany, but still its gateway

Madame de Sévigné (1626–1696)

Marie de Rabutin-Chantal, Marquise de Sévigné, spent a considerable part of her life, from a need to economise rather than from choice, at the château of Les Rochers, outside Vitré. She relieved the tedium of provincial life by describing its *beau monde* wittily, with the same sharp observation she brought to her descriptions of court life when she was at Versailles and Paris. Her letters to her daughter, the Comtesse de Grignan, left posterity a vivid portrait of events, customs and manners in the reign of Louis XIV.

During the reprisals which followed the revolt of the Bonnets Rouges against oppressive taxes she described how local people flocked together in the fields and threw themselves on their knees crying 'Mea culpa', the only phrase they knew the French would understand. 'There's no end to the hangings of these poor Bas-Bretons; they ask for a drink and for it to be over and done with.'

Madame de Sévigné was widowed when the Marquis, whom she married in 1644, died in a duel. She did not marry again and brought up her two children with the help of her uncle, the Abbé Christophe de Coulanges. She inherited the 15th-century château with its round pointed turrets, adding an octagonal chapel for which she designed the furniture. Her greatest pride were the gardens which she made with local workmen led by Jacques Pilois, whose conversation she preferred, she once wrote, to that of any *chevalier* at the Breton Parliament in Rennes. She found beauty and sadness in watching the trees grow straight and tall and enjoyed being in the thick of pruning and felling among her workmen.

Her prudent and frugal soul was outraged by the excesses of the ruling class to which she belonged. When the States met at Vitré, she wrote to her daughter that roast joints were removed as though untouched and 'as for the pyramids of fruit, the doors should have been made higher to let them through'. She was glad to return to what she called '*ma solitude*' at Les Rochers, her needlework and letter writing in a room with a view of her alleys of limes radiating into the woods beyond. Her room, the *cabinet vert*, is open to visitors, together with the chapel. Les Rochers today is much as it was in Madame de Sévigné's day, with the addition of an 18th-century stable block.

---

total contrast to the frenetic bustle of Le Mont St. Michel, quiet even in July, with little traffic. Senior citizens in floppy Breton berets smile and say 'Bonjour' as they pass. The tourist office organises free guided tours, departing from the Maison du Tourisme at 9pm every evening, but the commentaries are in French only.

The N12 runs directly to Rennes from Fougères, passing near the famous battlefield of St. Aubin du Cormier. It was here on 28 July 1488 that Duke François II fought, and lost, his final battle against the French overlords. There is little to see but a plaque marking the spot amidst the stately forests to the north-east of the regional capital. History is more visible along the alternative route via the D798, D178, D857 and N157 passing through fortress towns along the banks of the Vilaine.

Vitré is the most dramatic of these places, its grey-brown bulk filling the horizon as you round a bend in the road. The Tertre Noir, a hill to the north, gives a commanding view of the château and the old town, particularly when its round towers, spires and ramparts are silhouetted against a setting sun. The Paris to Brest railway was carved through Vitré in the 19th century without a great deal of regard for preservation of its medieval architecture. None the less, enough survives to make a stroll through the narrow, cobbled medieval streets near the railway station a memorable experience. The Promenade beneath the ramparts looks over the valley of the River Vilaine. The 15th-century Church of Notre-Dame has an exterior pulpit from which priests harangued passers-by. During the Wars of Religion these dissertations were apt to turn into fierce theological arguments with the Calvinists who occupied the house on the opposite side of the street.

The best view of the castle is from the garden off the rue d'Embas from which the rue Beaudrairie leads to the massive drawbridge and gate. It dates from the 11th century and is built in the form of a triangle. From the Middle Ages it was the home of the powerful Montmorency-Laval family, but by the beginning of the 19th century the castle was little but a ruin. It was bought by the municipal authorities for a token sum and in the early 1900s a mock Gothic town hall was built inside the walls. The St. Laurent Tower houses a museum which includes an exceptional set of 16th-century Limoges enamels in their original frames.

The Brittany States (États) met on occasion at Vitré and were subjected to the scrutiny of Madame de Sévigné, whose château of **Les Rochers-Sévigné**

The 11th-century castle at Vitré is in the form of a triangle

is buried in the woods 6.5km to the south on the D88, surrounded by the flowerbeds that provide a rare, living reconstruction of a 17th-century manorial park.

The distinctive octagonal church of **Châteaubourg**, on the River Vilaine between Vitré and Rennes, can be glimpsed from the N157-E50 autoroute which bypasses this ancient town. If there is time, a drive through the byroads is rewarding, with perhaps a call at the village of **Champeaux** where the Renaissance church has brilliant stained glass made in Rennes and canopied choir stalls. The mausolea of the Espinays, an old Breton family who lived in a nearby château, are to be found here.

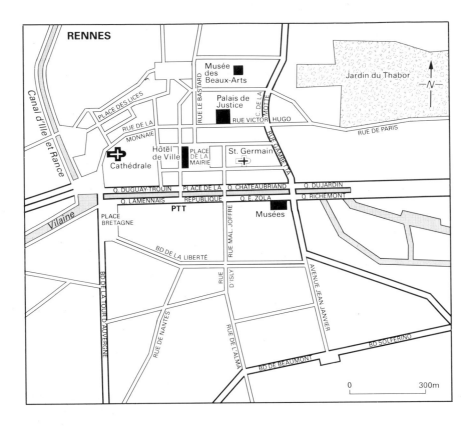

Rennes

The great River Vilaine flows through the heart of Brittany's capital, the *quais* on either bank lined with classical buildings. **Rennes** is a handsome city, accustomed to power. From the time of the Duchess Anne it was the seat of the Breton *Parlement* and today, with the transfer of its ancient rival Nantes to a separate neighbouring region, it is the undisputed capital of Brittany and of the *département* of Ille-et-Vilaine. Like Redon, Rennes took its name from the Redonnes, a Gaulish tribe conquered by the Romans. As it stood at the confluence of two rivers, the Vilaine and the Ille, the Romans developed it, making it the junction of three of their highways. To protect this strategic hub, they fortified it with stone walls and courses of Roman bricks which gave Rennes the more poetic name of Urbs Rubra, or Rose-red City.

Little survives of the Roman City and the central area was almost totally destroyed in the great fire which burned for six days over Christmas 1720. Seasonal supplies of meat and fuel in almost every house aided the spread of the blaze and by the time heavy rain brought it under control something like 900 buildings had been gutted. Robelin and Gabriel rebuilt the devastated area to a grid plan of streets and squares with buildings of attractive simplicity. This graceful 18th-century heart is surrounded by a medieval jumble of cobbled streets and half-timbered houses that survived the fire, which lies within an outer ring of 20th-century development including two universities engaged in the most advanced electronic teaching, an automated car factory, avenue after avenue of offices named after various EEC countries, and twin 30-storey blocks of flats aptly called Les Jumelles.

Driving is such in Rennes that the best advice one can give is to abandon the car in the first available parking space and explore on foot. There is much to see and the residents are unfailingly courteous and helpful with directions. The most notable building open to visitors in the place du Palais, right at the centre of things, is the Palais de Justice. Built between 1618 and 1655, it somehow managed to avoid being burned down in the Great Fire, and is still in use today for court hearings. Two loggias, high in the walls of the Grande Chambre du Parlement de la Bretagne among the gilded cornices and rich tapestries, were reserved for ladies— Madame de Sévigné was among those who used this vantage point to observe the *beau monde*. The Hôtel de Ville

There are plenty of outdoor cafés from which to watch the world of Rennes go by

built by Gabriel in 1734 after the fire is in the nearby place de la Mairie.

The Tabor Gardens, just a short walk from the place du Palais, are among the finest in France and need no man-made embellishment. Originally part of the Benedictine monastery of St. Melaine, and presumably named after the biblical Mount Tabor, they are the pride of Rennes, a former winner of the Concours National des Villes et Villages Fleuries.

The most prominent feature of le vieux Rennes is the Cathedral of St. Pierre, started in 1540 and completed 20 years before the fire. Its rather bleak 19th-century interior suggests little of the glory of successive Dukes of Brittany who came here to be crowned and passed in procession through the fortified Mordelaise Gate. Much more attractive, the church of St. Germain near the river has some beautiful stained glass in the east window and a gilded baldacchino over the altar. Opposite, on the south bank of the river, a graceful 19th-century building houses two fine museums. Beaux-Arts on the first floor has pottery from Rennes, Quimper and Dinan and the paintings of the malouin painter Jean-Julien Lemordant, who during his long life (1878-1968)

reflected the little-changing patterns around him. The Musée de Bretagne on the ground floor deals with the geology of the Promontory and has a fascinating collection of documents from the time of the Duchess Anne and of the Papier Timbre tax revolt of 1675. A large section is devoted to traditional Breton peasant costume and furniture such as the lit-clos (box bed), banc-coffre (bench-cum-chest) and table huche (table combined with a larder). Audio-visual presentations are a regular feature of the museum.

A fleeting visit to Rennes leaves the impression that it is more French than Breton even though the rue de la Monnaie on the edge of the medieval quarter is a reminder that it once had its own mint. Tourists sit elbow to elbow with office workers at open-air café tables or in the crêperies at lunchtime, washing down over-stuffed galettes and tarte au pommes with cider. A glance through the pages of Ouest France, the daily paper published from this city since the Liberation summer of 1944, will be enough to convince most visitors that in this most conservative of French regions, the Breton way of life is more than holding its own.

5
From Rennes to the Côte d'Amour

Rennes to Nantes

South-east from Rennes the citadel frontier with France stretches all the way to Nantes, its former rival as the capital of Brittany. **Châteaugiron** stands guard ominously on route D463. In 1592 the Duke of Mercoeur stormed this fortified town and hanged the whole garrison. Where the D463 meets the D178 running south from Fougères and Vitré, the little country town of **La Guerche-de-Bretagne** has memories of an often violent past. It featured in a 15th-century equivalent of the St. Nazaire raid of World War II when the Duke of Somerset captured it. He had landed at Cherbourg at the head of an 8,000-strong army and marched south into Brittany. In the previous century Bertrand du Guesclin had a castle here. This was eventually destroyed in the 18th century but the 13th-century Collegiate Church, rebuilt in the 15th and 16th centuries, survives. It is worth visiting for its Renaissance glass, sculptured choir stalls and misericords representing the seven deadly sins. Deep in the woods near La Guerche is the Roche-aux-Fées (Fairies' Rock) not just one but a collection of massive stones forming a megalithic monument, much visited by courting couples when there is a new moon.

Châteaubriant, 55km south of Rennes on the D163 and the D178, has the most impressive of castles, today the headquarters of the *Sous-préfecture*. The bureaucrats are sharing the accommodation with the ghosts of a sometimes turbulent past. The author François-René de Chateaubriand claimed descent from the Counts of Châteaubriant, one of whom, Jean de Laval, built the Renaissance château in the 16th century facing an earlier medieval structure. He brought his child bride, the eleven-year-old Françoise de Foix, here to keep her away from the temptations of Paris. But the king managed to get hold of the code word used by the Count to summon his wife and sent a message to the château.

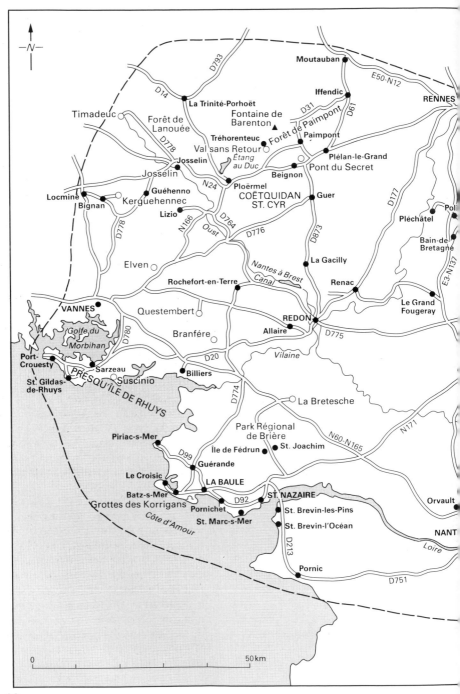

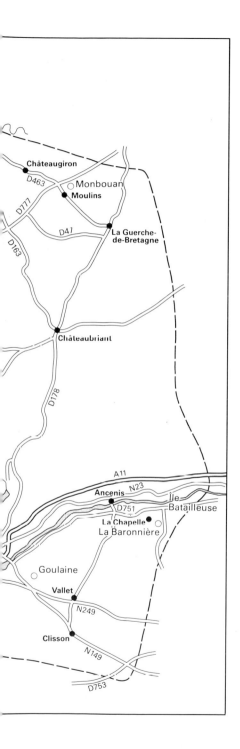

Françoise dutifully answered it and became the king's mistress. When he had tired of her, the king sent her back to Châteaubriant, where she died in 1537, the year that the castle was completed. Some accounts have it that her husband, having completed the new château for her, actually murdered her for her unfaithfulness. A stone plaque inside the walls commemorates an even grimmer piece of more recent history: it marks the spot where, in October 1941, 27 local hostages were put in front of a firing squad in retaliation for the killing of Colonel Holtz, the commander of the German garrison at Nantes. A monument to these heroes of the Resistance stands beside the N171, the road to Laval, just outside Châteaubriant.

The E3-N137 autoroute from Rennes to Nantes slices straight through a wooded landscape dotted with fortified manor houses and ruined castles such as Motte du Coudray and Motte du Véréal of which nothing but the *motte* or defensive mound remains. The towers and buildings, usually of wood, were destroyed. The busy trunk road bypasses charming country towns such as **Bain-de-Bretagne** and **Le Grand-Fougeray**, where only the keep of a once substantial frontier fortress survives.

Although **Nantes** is no longer officially a part of Brittany, spiritually and historically it cannot be separated. During the Middle Ages it vied with Rennes as the capital of the Duchy and it was the Dukes of Brittany who began its great château in the mid-15th century. Today it houses a variety of museums, one of them, the Musée d'Art Populaire Régional, containing collections as good as those at Rennes of Breton peasant dress, traditional furniture and

Half-timbered medieval houses survived the violent past of La Guerche-de-Bretagne

household equipment. The Musée des Salorges is devoted to the 'Commerce Triangulaire' by which Nantes, like Bristol, prospered as a seaport in the 17th and 18th centuries. The sailing ships depicted in the models here carried manufactured goods from France to the coast of West Africa, where they took on board a human cargo of natives to be sold into slavery on the plantations of the West Indies, returning with sugar cane from those plantations to feed the refineries of Nantes. The mighty Loire, the longest river in France, was a natural highway long before then and Nantes owed its importance to its situation only 55km from the mouth of that river. It was originally named after the Gaulish tribe of the Namnetes, whose main settlement it was, and who, along with their allies, the Veneti, were conquered by Julius Caesar. During its

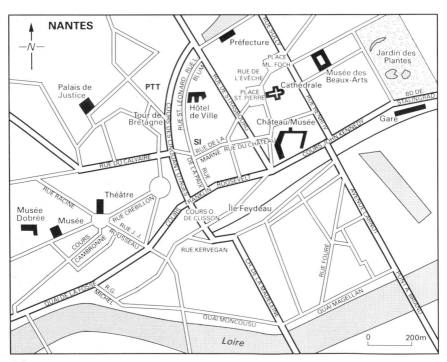

Roman period it was the capital of Armorica but when the Romans left the river brought in successive waves of marauding Norsemen. When they were finally routed in 937, Nantes became the capital of the victor, Alain Barbe-Torte, and as the centuries passed developed as a centre of trade with the outside world.

Today's city of nearly a quarter of a million people has an ultra-modern university built in huge white slabs but is still recognisably a port, with cranes and warehouses and attendant sugar refineries, canneries, chemical and engineering plants, and a shipper of Muscadet and Gros Plant wines from the vineyards in the surrounding countryside. Like Brest and Lorient it suffered heavy damage in the closing stages of World War II and the rebuilding since then included Le Corbusier's Cité Radieuse, followed by the familiar late 20th-century pattern of high-rise accommodation and offices such as the Tour de Bretagne in the city centre and multi-lane motorways that are jammed as soon as they are built. Tributaries of the Loire were turned into underground pipes with roads on top. For all that, Nantes still offers the visitor much to see and enjoy once one has penetrated the mysteries of its one-way traffic system.

The place to start exploring Nantes is the castle which dominates the very centre where the Gauls and the Romans had their towns and cannot be missed. When Henry IV came here in 1598 to sign the Edict of Nantes giving personal and religious freedom to Protestants as well as Catholics he made no attempt at disguising that he was impressed by the edifice erected by the Dukes of Brittany. There are some remains of an earlier medieval castle including a single tower called the Vieux Donjon but most of the fortifications that survive were begun by Duke Jean V and Duke François II and carried forward by the latter's daughter, Duchess Anne. It was she who built the horse-shoe shaped Tour du Fer à Cheval and the Tour de la Couronne d'Or with the Italianate loggias from which the ladies of the court could view tournaments in the tilting yard below.

The Cathedral of St. Pierre, also 15th-century but not completed until just under a century ago, is no more than a two-minute walk from the château. It was badly damaged during the Liberation of 1944 and again by a severe fire in 1972 but today its exceptionally high vaulted nave (35m) has been restored to its original glory. The Renaissance tomb of Duke François II and his wife which depicts them lying on a slab of white marble is said to be among the best examples of its kind. The heart of Duchess Anne was believed to be buried here, too, but the

King Henry IV of France was much impressed by the castle of the Dukes of Brittany at Nantes

La Roche-aux-Fées is a trysting place for courting couples (see page 59)

gold casket, when opened, contained nothing. It is kept in the Musée Dobrée in the place Jean V, which consists of three buildings built at different times over five centuries including the present. It presents a fascinating tableau of Nantes, and therefore of Breton, history. The Musée des Beaux Arts, a short walk from the cathedral in the direction of the Jardin des Plantes, is not particularly relevant to Brittany but is worth visiting for its miscellaneous collection of paintings from many countries of various periods.

Jules Verne, who was born in Nantes in 1828, is best remembered by his novels but a museum of his life and work is at 3 rue de l'Hermitage. There is also a statue of him in the Jardin des Plantes which has very pretty gardens

and a conservatory. Nantes is a city of flowers and the Floralies Internationales has been held regularly in the Parc de la Beaujoire on the outskirts of the city on the banks of the River Erdre.

Nantes has an array of elegant shops, many of them in the broad Cours des Cinquante Otages, which commemorates the hostages who were shot by the Germans in reprisal for the murder of the garrison commander here, and there is a tall copper monument bearing their names down by the River Erdre. The Resistance was strong here. Beyond the place Royale with its dramatic fountain, the narrow rue Crebillon provides more window shopping and a covered arcade called the Passage Pommeraye, a 19th-century extravaganza of decorative glazing and ironwork lavishly restored, leads off it. The Grand Théâtre in Plas Graslin is 18th-century with a neo-classical portico and La Cigale café nearby evokes the Belle Époque with its glazed tiles and ornately engraved mirrors while offering a menu for less than 60 francs.

On the way back to the castle lies the Cours Cambronne, a traffic-free square of fine houses dominated by a statue of the nantais general it is named after, with his rallying call to the Imperial Guard at Waterloo inscribed on the plinth. Translated, it reads 'The Guard dies but does not surrender'. However, the well-known *mot de Cambronne* is the five-letter French word that he uttered when called upon to surrender to the British. Further on, the Île Feydeau (no longer an island since new roads swallowed it up) retains none the less its rue Kervégan, lined with 18th-century town houses of the rich slave-traders with their quiet courtyards and galleried staircases. Not far from here in rue Foure is one of the best places to eat in Nantes, Les Maraîchers, but it is small, heavily booked and very expensive. Much cheaper, but also very good, is Le Colvert in rue Armand-Brossard. If dining in Nantes, the opportunity of sampling its native sauce, *beurre blanc* (see Recipes), should not be missed.

Until the 1960s and the transfer of Loire-Atlantique to the new region of the Pays de la Loire, Brittany extended south of the river and along its banks inland as far as **Ingrandes**, where smuggling used to take place across the river between the Bretons and the people of Anjou on the southern side. This most scenic stretch of the Loire, with its fine châteaux and vineyards, is dealt with in detail in the companion volume in this

series, *The Loire Valley*, by Arthur and Barbara Eperon, but this book cannot omit a mention of its place in Breton history and culture. The A11 autoroute from Angers to Nantes, and its equally busy companion the N23, parallel the unhurried river, while the 'modernised' N249 to Vallet and beyond charges through Muscadet country with barely a chance to get off to visit historic family vineyards such as the Château du Cléray. The D751, which wiggles its way along the south bank of the river offers enchanting views and relatively sane traffic conditions. Between the sleepy old river town of **Champtoceaux** and Ingrandes the road is sometimes a corniche along a steeply wooded hillside with the Loire at the bottom of the gorge and sometimes a winding ribbon across gently rolling meadows but nearly always attractive.

Ancenis, whose sailmakers were once the most famous in Brittany, rises in terraces on the steep north bank of the river on the other side of a suspension bridge. Today the town's major activities are pig dealing and wine; it is the home of Les Vignerons de la Noëlle (tel 40.98.92.72) whose products are widely sold in Britain. To reach their huge building on the ring road, turn right immediately after crossing the bridge from the D763 to taste and buy wines from all over the Loire Valley. Red, white and rosé Coteaux d'Ancenis wines are less well known, inexpensive and worth trying. Returning to the D751, heading east on the southern side of the river, the road passes through a succession of charming villages to **St. Florent-le-Vieil** with its commanding hilltop view of the **Île Batailleuse**, a base in the 9th century for the maurauding Norsemen who came up the river

65

Heloise and Abelard

The affair of a teacher of theology with a student 20 years his junior has inspired love stories beyond number and is as poignant today as it was when it took place 900 years ago. He set it down late in life in his own *Historia Calamitatum* (The Story of My Misfortunes).

Peter Abelard was born in Le Pallet, between Nantes and Clisson, in 1079 and fell in love with Heloise, a niece of one of the canons of Notre Dame who gave him lodging in Paris. When Heloise gave birth to a son, the couple married, although against her better judgement 'Who can concentrate on thoughts of scripture and philosophy and be able to endure babies crying...?' Abelard's solution was that his wife should enter a convent but he paid a terrible price at the hands of her relatives—they castrated him, provoking the public lamentations of his loyal followers, disciples and clerks.

Abelard became a monk at St. Denis while Heloise stayed in the convent. Later, c.1126, he accepted against his will the post of Abbot of St. Gildas-de-Rhuys in the wilds of southern Brittany, where he was even more miserable. Yet he was able to found the convent of the Paraclète at Troyes and install his beloved Heloise as Abbess. His unconventional views on the Trinity brought him into conflict with St. Bernard of Clairvaux when he returned to teaching in Paris towards the end of his life and he composed a number of hymns in Latin, some of which are sung to this day. He died in 1142 and Heloise survived him by 20 years. They were buried alongside one another at the Paraclète before being moved to a single sarcophagus at the cemetery of Père-Lachaise, Paris. *The Letters of Abelard and Heloise* (published as a Penguin Classic) bear witness to their abiding love for each other against all odds.

from the Atlantic in their dragon-headed longboats, pillaging, burning, looting, raping and murdering as they went. The island splits the river in twain at this point, a natural fortress used as such by the invaders for 80 years until they were defeated and driven out by the first Breton warrior hero, Alain Barbe-Torte.

The best Muscadet wine comes from Sèvre-et-Maine, south-east of Nantes: take the N149 (*not* the N249) and continue on the D756 towards **La Chapelle-Heulin**, just beyond which is the **Château de la Noë de Bel Air** (tel 40.33.92.72) where the Comte de Malestroit's family have lived and made wine for more than two centuries. The Sauvion family's **Château de Cleray** is not far away on the other side of the village of **Vallet** (take the D756 as far as La Chalousière, then the D106 over the N249, and then you will soon see the sign for the château). Apart from these great houses there are numerous small growers in these parts displaying boards: 'Dégustation et Vente Directe' where wines can be tasted and bought on the spot without formality. If you stay on the N149 instead of making a detour to the châteaux you will see many of these boards, especially around **La Haie-Fouassière** which is also the home of the Maison des Vins du Pays Nantais. **Le Pallet**, where Peter Abelard the tragic victim of the immortal love story of Heloise and Abelard was born, is just 9km down the road and another place to taste and buy the best Muscadet. The N149 leads directly to **Clisson**, birthplace of Olivier de Clisson, who switched his allegiance from the English to the French after losing an eye in the last great battle of the Breton War of Succession in 1364. His zeal made him known as 'the butcher of the English' and in 1380 he was appointed Constable of France. He built the spectacular riverside castle at Josselin (see later this chapter), today in a much better state of preservation than the family château here, which lies in ruins. The town itself, at the confluence of the rivers Maine and Sèvre in the heart of the wine country, was burned to the ground in 1794 and rebuilt subsequently. Upstream on the Sèvre Nantaise (16km on the N149, turning right on to the D753) at **Tiffauges** is the ruined castle of another old Breton warrior, infamous as the original for Bluebeard, the wife-killer Gilles de Rais, marshal of France at 25, fought at the side of Joan of Arc at the Siege of Orleans before turning to the black arts after her death. He was executed at Nantes for mass murder in 1140. His lands (the domaines of Ingrandes and Chantoce) were confiscated by Duke Jean V of Brittany and given to his younger son, the ill-fated Gilles de Bretagne.

Nantes to Vannes

Nantes is the gateway to Southern Brittany from the Loire Valley. The arterial N165 which carries the vast amount of westward traffic should be endured only for as long as it takes to get to a convenient turning off for the golden beaches of the beguilingly named Côte d'Amour or the mysteries of the marshlands of la Grande Brière, a regional park, which lies just inland from **St. Nazaire** at the mouth of the Loire estuary. St. Nazaire is a shipbuilding town, hardly designed for tourists, almost totally destroyed by air raids and bombardments during World War II when it was an important German U-boat base and rebuilt since in an unlovely concrete functional style. Its memories of the war, proudly recorded, are inevitably sad. The troopship *Lancastria* went down in the estuary after repeated dive-bombing with the loss of 3,000 British Tommies being evacuated from St. Nazaire a couple of weeks after Dunkirk in the summer of 1940. Less than two years later a daring Commando raid launched from Britain put the name of St. Nazaire back in the headlines with further heavy loss of life.

In World War I, the Canadians disembarked here in 1915 on their way to the trenches, followed two years later by the first American 'doughboys'. In peacetime the docks of St. Nazaire have been busy with the construction of vast passenger liners: both the *Normandie* and the *France* and the tradition continues with a late 20th-century burst of activity catering for the leisure industry in warmer waters than the Atlantic. In 1987 Chantiers de l'Atlantique at

St. Nazaire launched the largest passenger ship ever built, the 70,000-tonne *Sovereign of the Seas* for the Royal Caribbean cruise line. Soaring above the shipyard, a spectacular 3,356m-long suspension bridge between two red and white striped pylons crosses the estuary enabling drivers (for the payment of a toll) to travel directly from Brittany into the Vendée, or to the Atlantic resorts of St. Brevin and Pornic, by-passing the congestion around Nantes.

The little resort of **St. Marc-sur-Mer** lies on the western outskirts of St. Nazaire, to all appearances unchanged since Jacques Tati filmed his minor masterpiece *Monsieur Hulot's Holiday* here in the 1950s. I half expected to see M. Hulot in shorts and sun hat coming down the steps of the Hôtel de la Plage with that curious gait of his and to hear the continual, haunting squeak of the swing-door to the kitchen but I was disappointed on both counts. The food and the service bore no relation to that depicted in the film although some of the clients bore an almost uncanny resemblance to characters in it. The clean sands almost on the doorstep face south across the open sea to the Pointe de St. Gildas and the unruffled coastal setting of lighthouses, a fort, a semaphore point and a cannon is a tribute to the innate conservatism of provincial France. Whatever the bureaucrats may say or do, St. Marc-sur-Mer remains the archetypal seaside resort of Southern Brittany and there is a well-equipped campsite, Municipal de l'Ève (tel 40.91.90.65), just a kilometre east of the village with easy access to the beach.

The interior of Nantes Cathedral possesses rare grace (see page 63)

La Grande Brière

The Nantes-Brest motorway passes to the north, and just to the south lie the smiling seaside resorts of the Côte d'Amour and the clamorous shipyards of St. Nazaire, yet the Brière regional park covers 40,000 hectares of completely natural, unspoiled country. Its heart is La Grande Brière, a large area of silent marshland crossed by few humans other than reed cutters and duck shooters and the occasional tourists poled along in a *chaland* or punt by a local guide; yet men have lived here since prehistoric times. There is a classic novel *La Brière* written by Alphonse de Châteaubriant and published in the 1920s which captures the strange, brooding quality of the place and the loneliness of the people living there, so near to civilisation yet so far from it. It is owned by the people of the 21 communes surrounding it, from St. Nazaire to the smallest village, a right that was granted in 1462 by Duke François II of Brittany and is jealously guarded to this day. Until as recently as 1950 peat-cutting was the major occupation of the Briërons but with the formation of the regional park tourism seems to have taken over. There is even a small museum in a former lock-keeper's cottage—the Maison de l'Eclusier in a small village called **Rosé** and in August there's a festival with all kinds of waterborne contests and games. Despite this, La Grande Brière remains a well-kept secret, with no signs pointing to it and no obvious appearance of commercialisation. The main village is **St. Joachim**, on the D50, a scenically interesting route between Missilac and St. Nazaire which runs along the eastern side of the marsh, which is dissected by a grid of straight canals. The administration is at **Île de Fedrun**, one of the islands among the reeds surrounding St. Joachim, in a conversion of two thatched cottages. The Auberge du Parc here serves specialities prepared from Brière eels and duck. Whitewashed cottages with thatched roofs stand in well-tended kitchen gardens, each with its own channel to the waterway. However, many of the roofs are covered in moss or have fallen in completely, giving the village a somewhat desolate air even on a fine summer's day.

The St. Nazaire Raid

During World War II, St. Nazaire, with its facilities and location in the Bay of Biscay, was an important German submarine base. It also had the world's largest drydock that prewar had handled trans-Atlantic liners such as the *Normandie*. On 28 March 1942 it was the target of the sauciest raid since Drake, codenamed 'Operation Chariot'. An obsolete destroyer, HMS *Campbelltown*, packed with high explosive, rammed the gates of the *forme écluse* at the Bassin de St. Nazaire putting it out of action while Commandos with blackened faces swarmed ashore to inflict further damage. The Allies paid a terrible price, however. Out of 611 taking part, only 242 returned to England, while the Germans took savage reprisals against local people. A granite column beside the harbour pier lists the dead.

A quiet coastal road (D292) continues westward from St. Marc to meet up with dual-carriageway at **Pornichet**, transformed from a salt-marsh workers' village to a fashionable 19th-century watering place when it was discovered by writers from Paris. Its bohemian style was enhanced by the building of a racecourse, which still flourishes. Fast hydrojets (Vedettes Rapides) operate from the *gare maritime* here (tel 40.61.62.63) to offshore islands such as Belle-Île and Houat. Pornichet marks the extremity of a 9km scimitar of south-facing sands washed by Atlantic breakers and sheltered by pine trees—**La Baule** 'la belle'—the most beautiful beach in France according to its municipal champions. Certainly, on a fine day the bronzed bodies arrayed on the beach, the brilliant colours of the sea and the sails of the windsurfers (and the wetsuits of those who sail them with such panache) make a very pretty postcard. But of course in high season the place is packed and the traffic roaring along the esplanade sends up such a fug that it's surprising it doesn't kill off even those hardy maritime pines planted so

farsightedly a hundred years ago to keep the dunes in their place.

Despite the crowds and the stalls selling '*Frites, sandwichs*' (sic) at exorbitant prices La Baule manages to stay chic. The Deauville of the West, it retains something of its 1930s snob-appeal when Aston Martin 1½-litre Le Mans tourers were lined up on the gravel outside the Hôtel Hermitage while their drivers recovered from the gruelling course of the 24-hour race with champagne, fresh foie gras and baccarat at the casino nearby. In mid-August the vintage Hispano-Suizas and Isotta-Fraschinis rally in the town for a *concours d'élégance*. The Hermitage is the very grandest of hotels and the Castel Marie-Louise in the esplanade Casino serves possibly the finest food in Brittany but La Baule has a range of hotels and restaurants to suit all tastes and pockets. The tourist office at 8 place Victoire (tel 40.24.34.44) keeps full information on vacancies.

Overleaf: Punts or chalands are the only way to explore the marshes of the Brière

71

La Baule is an international sporting centre, playing host to tennis, golf and showjumping championships, catamaran and windsurfing festivals. Montoir Airport, which it shares with St. Nazaire, is 24km away and has scheduled flights to Paris. There are more than 100 tennis courts, four horse riding clubs, an 18-hole golf course at St. Denac and numerous sailing schools as well as aqualung diving and deep sea fishing. **Le Pouliguen** occupies the opposite end of La Baule's celebrated beach to Pornichet. They became resorts at about the same period of the 19th century and Le Pouliguen's fishing boats rub fenders with gleaming yachts in the little harbour where fish and crustaceans are piled on the quay. It prides itself on being a fishing and leisure port at the same time and there are plenty of shops and cafés in the narrow streets.

The harbour is at the mouth of the canal which carries the tides in and out of an enormous jigsaw of clay banks known as the **Marais Salants**. The seawater decants into reservoirs and is finally captured in *oeillets* where evaporation takes place, leaving deposits of salt. Along the thin neck of land protecting the saltpans from the sea is an intriguing Sentier des Douaniers full of creeks, caves and strangely shaped rocks. The Grotte des Korrigans (korrigans being the Breton version of leprechauns) lies just beneath the corniche road D45 which leads to **Batz-Sur-Mer** a 10th-century granite town standing sentinel between ocean and marsh. There are 15th-century ruins and the 17th-century church tower of St. Guénolé which is a landmark for kilometres

Previous page: The sun rises over one of Europe's most beautiful beaches at La Baule

/4

around. Honoré de Balzac stayed here while working on his monumental sequence of novels the *Comédie humaine* which depicted so many aspects of 19th-century French life. **Le Croisic**, at the tip of the peninsula 10km from the centre of La Baule, is another bustling fishing port-cum-marina where each day lobster, crayfish, crab and shrimp are landed on the stone jetty. Those who prefer to catch their own can fish with a line for bass, pollack and bream. The quays and narrow streets are lined with houses of the 15th to 17th centuries and there's an aquarium and marine museum. The road inland (D774) runs across the marshes to the village of **Saillé** where the traditional house of a salt maker, the maison des Paludiers, is preserved as a museum.

The D774 continues inland to **Guérande** which is set on a plateau commanding the marshes and is surrounded by almost perfect circular ramparts with ten towers. When built by the Dukes of the 13th and 15th centuries it was protected by a moat, long since filled in and replaced by a circular road. There are four fortified gates into the town, the most flamboyant of which, Porte St. Michel, contains a museum of regional folklore. The spire of the 17th-18th-century church of St. Aubin rises above this quaint old town within its encircling wall like a spindle at the hub of a wheel. Balzac describes Guérande in his novel *Béatrix*. There are wonderfully scenic roads from here and from Saillé westwards across the marshes to **la Turballe**, where the blue and white sardine boats sail in amidst screeching clouds of gulls, and on around the coast to **Lerat** and **Piriac-sur-Mer**, traditional fishing ports with 17th-century timber-framed houses, natural havens for yachtsmen and anglers. The coastline is jagged and rocky, with little beaches and inlets and meandering by-roads all the way round to the estuary of the Vilaine.

The direct route from Nantes to Vannes skirts the northern edge of the Grande Brière. At **Pontchâteau** there is a huge calvary, an indication perhaps that you are in Brittany whatever the powers-that-be may say. At **Missillac** 10km further on (the actual border) stands a 14th-century Renaissance château of unsurpassed loveliness with its cluster of round pointed turrets. This is La Bretesche, the home of the famous golf course laid out amidst the woods surrounding a lake. What used to be the château's farm and stables is now a very comfortable hotel. Eleven kilometres on into Morbihan, the dual carriageway of route N165 flies over the gorge of the River Vilaine with a spectacular view flashing past the car windows. It is well worth pausing at **La Roche-Bernard**, the riverside town below the bridge. Noted for its shipyards in the 17th century, it is now a port of call for pleasure boats, yachts and motor cruisers on the inland waterway that stretches north all the way to Dinan and the Rance estuary.

The crooked medieval streets lined with half-timbered houses tell of La Roche-Bernard's long history. Its mayor refused to shout 'Long live the King' when ordered to do so by the Chouan opponents of the Revolution, calling out instead 'Long live the Republic!' This interesting little town is so well endowed with good, moderately priced hotels that it is worth thinking about making an overnight stop there or at least having a meal. Just downriver is

the **Arzal** barrage, a base for pleasure boats such as the floating restaurant *Anne de Bretagne*.

Continuing along the N165 to Vannes, at **Muzillac** smart new housing developments are spreading like a rash over green countryside. At **Le Guerno** on the D20 road from Redon, Branfère Castle stand in a 50-hectare park where 2,000 birds and mammals, including scarlet ibis, wading birds and kangaroos, live in freedom amidst exotic plants and trees. Beyond Muzillac the D20 forks left to the Rhuys Peninsula, which remains a quiet backwater producing a wine that remains unknown outside its own boundaries. It forms the lower arm of the Gulf of Morbihan where the Veneti took on Julius Caesar's galleys and were defeated. When Peter Abelard was sent here against his will in the 12th century to be abbot at **St. Gildas-de-Rhuys** it was a wild region whose people spoke only Breton, a language unknown to him, and where the monks were 'beyond control and led a dissolute life which was well known to

Watermills still turn on the banks of the River Vilaine, a highway for pleasure boats and cruisers

There's a spectacular view from the bridge at La Roche-Bernard

all'. St. Gildas today is a pleasant holiday town reminiscent of Cornwall with its sands, rocks and dunes and an excellent camping ground. This seems apt as St. Gildas (born c.499) came from Cornwall and his bones lie in caskets in the Romanesque abbey church. Poor Abelard isn't commemorated at all.

The restored castle of **Suscinio**, a residence of the Dukes of Brittany from the 13th to the 15th centuries when the Rhuys peninsula was covered with forest rich with game, was wrecked during the Revolution. However, the sumptuous medieval floor of the ducal chapel survives. The castle stands at the edge of the Atlantic, so near to the sea that originally the tide rose and fell in its moat. The fairy Mélusine is said to haunt its subterranean tunnels. **Port-Navalo** and

Arzon stand at the very tip of the peninsula where a narrow passage provides the only outlet from the Gulf of Morbihan to the sea. They are traditionally sleepy little places enlivened only by the occasional arrival or departure of a pleasure boat, although there has been recent development of a popular new yachting resort called **Port-Crouesty** with holiday apartments and villas offering a range of leisure and sporting facilities including a newly laid out golf course.

The only town of any size on the Presqu'île de Rhuys is still **Sarzeau** which stands on the inner side facing the gulf. In the main square is a bust of its most famous son, playwright and novelist Alain-René Lesage (1668-1747), who wrote *Gil Blas*, a classic of

Breton literature. The church here has painted statues of two saints: Isidore in the garb of a peasant and Corneille (or Cornély) the patron saint of farm animals.

Rennes to Vannes

The main road (D177) south from Rennes to the Côte d'Amour has few diversions to offer until it reaches Redon, unless you wish to make a detour on by-roads to the west of Renac to visit the hamlet of **La Bataille** where Brittany first gained its independence from the Franks in 845. The railway, on the other hand, keeps company with the River Vilaine on its sinuous track across country to the sea, with wayside stations at little visited towns and villages. One such is **Langon**, which boasts the oldest complete building in Brittany, a 6th-century chapel honouring St. Agatha, who underwent a primitive masectomy and is the patron saint of nursing mothers. It stands opposite the village church but was probably a pagan shrine originally. Evidence of this comes from a latterly uncovered wall painting, in poor condition but showing Venus rising from the sea. A survival of Druidic rites stands on the open moor outside the village—the series of standing stones known as the Demoiselles de Langon.

Redon, at the junction of the Vilaine and the Nantes-Brest canal, several roads and the railway, is a busy town, full of character, a place to wander around, camera in hand. Its dominating feature is the church of St. Sauveur, all that remains of an abbey founded in the 9th century by Brittany's first 'home-ruler', Nominoë. It has a marvellous arcaded Romanesque lantern tower of granite and sandstone. Dating from the 12th century, it is probably the best example of this style to be found anywhere in Brittany. Opposite it and separated physically by a fire more than two centuries ago is the Gothic bell-tower. Redon's position at a crossroads is underlined by the railway level crossing at the side of the main square occupied by the church and the town hall, the juggernaut trucks thundering through its narrow streets and over its bridges, and the barges and boats passing through its array of navigation locks.

Redon is 42km inland from the barrage at Arzal and waterways radiate from here deep into the countryside. **Peillac**, 16km to the north-west, is off the beaten track. A lane leads from the village to a peaceful stretch of the River Oust-Nantes Canal where holiday cruisers and barges tie up for the night. There is a campsite run by the local commune on the canal bank. The village amidst fields of sunflowers and tiny hay meadows is completely unspoiled. There is even a *pissoir* after the style of *Clochemerle* just off the main street. Chez Antoine is a roadside inn with geranium-filled window boxes and a pretty *jardin d'agrément* with small white tables and chairs. The food is excellent and moderately priced. The Oust waterway continues through lovely countryside to **Malestroit** where boats accommodating from two to ten people can be hired, not to mention bicycles. The parish church of St. Gilles has the distinction of two naves, each in a different style, but the town is otherwise

Inland Waterways

Although Brittany is a boating and fishing paradise, attention is focused more often on its coastal creeks, estuaries and harbours than its inland waterways. Yet it has 1,100km of interconnected canals and rivers that no longer carry commercial traffic and provide delightful cruising away from the crowds to little visited places deep in the Argoat or interior. They admit boats with a draught of up to 1.2m. Apart from waterborne travel, the towpaths are easy-to-follow walking and cycling trails and many are still used as bridlepaths. The inland waterway network of Brittany is in two main sections.

The **Canal d'Ille-et-Rance et Vilaine** links the coasts of the Channel and the Atlantic from north to south, a total distance of 240km with 63 locks. This great waterway passes through some charming, unspoiled countryside that is not even seen from the main roads, as well as historic towns and cities such as **Dinan**, **Rennes** and **Redon**. There are tidal barrages at either end: at the northern end, the **Rance Dam** provides easy access to the lower reaches of that river and at the southern end the **Arzal Barrage**, completed in 1970, creates no less than 78km of non-tidal waterway, the longest in Western France.

The **Canal de Nantes à Brest** cuts straight down the middle of the peninsula, east to west, and although the middle section between **Pontivy** and **Carhaix** is now closed to traffic since the building of the Guerledan reservoir and dam near **Mur-de-Bretagne**, the rest of it is more than enough for a leisurely one- or two-week cruise. It runs north and west from **Nantes** via the River Erdre to the water crossroads of Redon, where it joins the River Oust heading west to **Josselin** where the riverside castle is one of the most photographed in France. From Pontivy in central Brittany, the river Blavet provides a route to the south coast at the former French East India Company port of **Lorient**. The navigable part of the Nantes-Brest Canal west of Carhaix to **Pont-Coblant** joins with the sinuous River Aulne on a long journey to the western extremities of Finistère, finally flowing into the Rade de Brest.

unremarkable. **Rochefort-en-Terre**, on the other hand, is forever being photographed because of its dolls' house architecture, little granite cottages strung along a ridge with a medieval castle and a 16th-century church as a backdrop. The main road to Vannes (D775) cuts between Rochefort-en-Terre and **Questembert** to the west. Despite being the site of the final his-

toric battle between Alain Barbe-Torte and the Norman invaders in 938, this is an unpretentious little market town, more noted these days for a restaurant, the Bretagne, which is rated by Michelin as 'being worth a detour'.

Argoat, the ancient word for Brittany's hinterland, means 'country of the woods' but there are scarcely any forests of any size remaining except for one 40km west of Rennes. **Paimpont**, a small market town with a medieval gate and a restored abbey church at the edge of a beautiful lake, to the north of the busy trunk route that leads to Ploërmel and on to the south coast, lies at the heart of the Forêt de Paimpont. Its ancient name was Brocéliande, a name that evokes the rites, spells and mysteries of the Druids and the court of King Arthur.

In the 8km between Plélan-le-Grand and Beignon, where the N24 crosses the River Aff at the Pont du Secret, is the trysting place of Sir Lancelot and Queen Guinevère. The magic fountain of Barenton is hidden amidst the oaks (see Box) to the north and a painting in the church at **Tréhorenteuc** on the western edge of the forest shows the Holy Grail appearing to King Arthur and his knights. The ghosts of Merlin the wizard and the witch Morgan and the Fay still haunt the Val sans Retour (Valley of No Return) nearby. There are panoramic views from the *haute forêt* over the Valley of the Fairies from which the village of **Concoret** takes its name and towards **Comper** where a stately château is reflected in the still waters of the large lake from which Sir Lancelot took his title du Lac. It's said that Merlin's Castle lies beneath its surface. The pink granite of the château claimed as the birthplace of the fairy Viviane and the ruins of a medieval castle make this an enchanted place to picnic or go fishing on a fine day.

Flanking the N24 as it continues towards Ploërmel is heathland used by the army for training its cadets in the use of tanks and other 20th-century armour, and a by-road to the south leads to Coëtquidan St. Cyr, the French equivalent of the British Army's Sandhurst College. **Ploërmel** is one of the larger towns of the Argoat. Severely damaged in World War II and rebuilt since, its chief interest to visitors lies in

The Fairy Spring

Merlin fell under the spell of the fairy Viviane, the Lady of the Lake, while he slept by a fountain in the Forest of Brocéliande. According to one of the many and various legends, to keep him she encased him inside the Merlin Stone which stands beside the Fairy Spring at Barenton. The path to it from the curiously named hamlet of Folle-Pensée (Mad Thought) near the village of Le Saudrais is signposted but difficult to follow. A compass is useful as the spring lies in a generally south-westerly direction. The **Perron de Merlin** (Merlin's Threshold) is the large square stone standing near the granite basin into which the spring flows.

It is said that if water from the Fairy Spring is sprinkled on the stone rain will fall. During a prolonged drought in 1835, the *Recteur* of Concoret (then called Konkored, or Valley of the Fairies) led a procession of his parishioners to the spring and splashed water on the stone using the cup that used to be attached to it by a chain. There is no clear record of what happened next although local folklore insists that the procedure never fails to make the heavens open.

the splendid lake Étang au Duc on its northern outskirts and the 16th-century church dedicated to its patron and founder of the 6th century, St. Armel.

But the most impressive piece of medieval architecture in Brittany is to be found 12km further along the N24 at **Josselin**: the castle built by Olivier de Clisson. However, the best approach to it is not by the highway but from the byroad that runs off to the left just beyond a granite monument to the fallen in the 'Battle of the Thirties' which stands on the central reservation between the dual carriageways. This leads to the back road which accompanies the River Oust towards the town. Even better, approach Josselin by boat and see the castle walls and their trio of towers rising at the riverside. The first castle on this site was attacked and destroyed by

The walls of the château at Josselin rise sheer from the River Oust

the English in the 12th century. It was de Clisson, the 'Butcher of the English', who raised the mighty walls sheer from the river in the late 14th century. Today a road intervenes but the waterside aspect of Josselin castle is still tremendous. It is hardly less impressive inside, where the Rohans, who became de Clisson's in-laws and own the place still, decorated every pinnacle and gable, doorway and balustrade with the most elaborate stone carving, living up to the family motto of ' *A plus*' or 'to excess'. This legend, entwined with the initial 'A' of the Duchess Anne and the crown of her husband, the King of France, recurs throughout the castle and is emblazoned above the fireplace in the Grand Salon in gold on red. In the stables 500 dolls of the famous Rohan family collection, with their accessories, are on display. For years after the Revolution, the château was allowed to fall into ruin until major restoration took place in the 19th century.

Just across the bridge from the castle, the Hôtel du Château makes a comfortable and moderately priced base for touring the area. Josselin is an attractive old town, its half-timbered houses adorned with flower-filled window boxes. Apart from the château, the basilica of Notre Dame du Roncier containing the tombs of Olivier de Clisson and his wife Marguerite de Rohan is worth visiting. The church gets its name from a 9th-century miracle when a peasant came across a bramble beside the River Oust which kept its leaves year round and in its centre a wooden figure of the Virgin. However many times the statue was removed it returned of its own accord to the bush and so eventually a chapel was built around it. The effigy was burned as an 'object of super-

Locks regulate this crossroads of Brittany waterways at Redon (see pages 77–8)

stition' by the Revolutionaries in 1789 (some fragments are kept in a reliquary) and a new statue was made in 1868. This is the centrepiece of the famous *pardon* of Notre Dame du Roncier on the second Sunday of September.

The countryside around Josselin repays the effort of exploration. To the north of the town, the remains of Roman camps lie hidden in the Forêt de Lanouée. To the east, near the banks of the tranquil Canal de Nantes à Brest, Trappist monks at the Abbaye de Tima-deuc silently welcome visitors with slides picturing their way of life and pro-duce their own cheese. To the west, towards Locminé at **Bignan**, the castle of Kerguehennec stands in a wooded park designed by the Buller brothers in

the 19th century. It is full of intriguing sculpture from many parts of the world. To the south, towards Vannes, before the small town of **St. Jean-Brévelay** which takes its name from the English archbishop St. John of Beverley, the low, wooded hills are dotted with megaliths and the village of **Guéhenno** has one of the few calvaries to be found in Haute Bretagne. It dates from 1550 and the tomb or ossuary is guarded by stone figures of soldiers. These are inti-mations of being on the mythical fron-tier of Basse Bretagne; the further west one travels into the Argoat the more Breton become the country and its people.

The Counter-Revolutionaries

The storming of the Bastille on 14 July 1789 put paid to the dream of Breton independence that had been kept alive for 250 years. Six months later the division of France into 87 *départements* effectively wiped the name of Brittany off the map. The confiscation of church endowments, the wholesale destruction of calvaries and chapels, the reign of terror in Nantes and the execution of Louis XVI all contributed to the disaffection of traditionalist Bretons who banded themselves together as Chouans, counter-revolutionaries. *Chat-huant*, the call of the screech owl, was their rallying signal.

They rallied first to a Breton aristocrat, the Marquis de la Rouerie, who paradoxically had fought in the American War of Independence alongside George Washington. Having exhausted himself winning support for an uprising in his home province he died of shock on hearing the news of the King's death by guillotine. Many of his own followers suffered a similar fate. The Chouan cause was taken up in Morbihan by Georges Cadoual, but was doomed to failure after he teamed up with two disgruntled aristocrats who landed with an expeditionary force from England on the coast at Carnac. They were driven back to the tip of the Quiberon peninsula, where they were trapped, as the Republican General Hoche put it succinctly, 'like rats'. Some escaped to the English fleet offshore but most were captured and shot in the Champ des Martyrs, a field outside Auray, birthplace of Cadoual. Their leader escaped to fight again six years later at the head of a royalist army in Brittany but again he was defeated and fled to England in a fishing boat. By now Napoleon was at the height of his power and Chouannerie was a lost cause; but that didn't deter Cadoual from landing in France with a plan to kidnap the just proclaimed Emperor Bonaparte. He was caught and put before a firing squad in Paris in June 1804.

Part Two:
Basse Bretagne

6
From Vannes to Quimper

Vannes to Quiberon

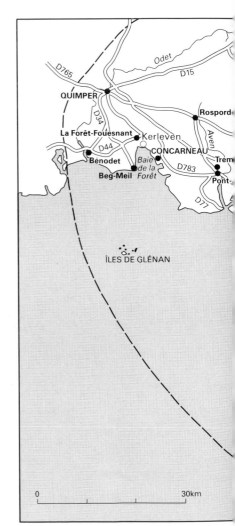

Vannes has a long history, having been in its time capital of a Gaulish tribe, the Veneti, and later of the Dukes of Brittany. It remains today a bustling market town and prefecture of the *département*, on the northern rim of the Gulf of Morbihan. It makes a good base for exploring this area, with a network of local bus services and boat trips to the islands in the gulf. The *promenade en bateau* from Vannes takes visitors around the Gulf of Morbihan which contains hundreds of islands, some submerged at low tide. The biggest are **Moines**, 6km long, and **Arz**, about half that size, wooded and quite beautiful. Round trips range from two hours to a whole day. Vedettes Vertes run gastronomical cruises in the restaurant boat *Navispace*. Both sea and river fishing is readily to hand. The walled town around the cathedral is a medieval gem, carefully restored over recent years with many of the narrow streets and little squares within the walls (called Intra Muros as at St. Malo) barred to motor traffic. The covered market beside the west front of the cathedral is called La Cohue (hubbub) and lives up to this name as the pancake sellers and purveyors of local handicrafts vie for the attention of the tourists who flock here in summer. The place des Lices, where two carved figureheads Vannes and his Wife leer mockingly from the wall of the House of Vannes, is crammed with stalls and people on market days. The

port, which ranges along a canal into the waters of the Gulf, comes to the foot of the ramparts, which while not as perfect as St. Malo's are extremely well-kept, with neat flower beds in the drained moat. The two surviving town gates, Porte-Prison at the northern end of the walls and Porte-Poterne at the other, have been restored, too. Below the latter are some unusual 16th-

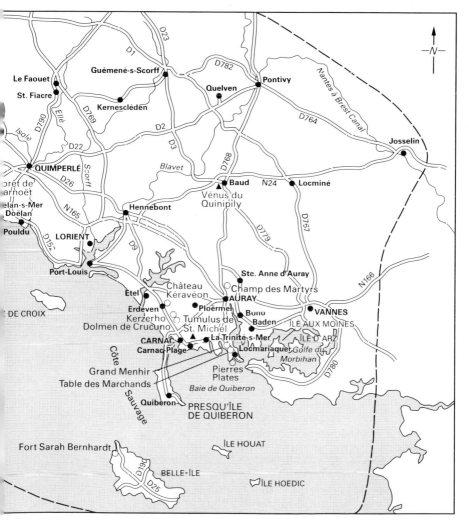

85

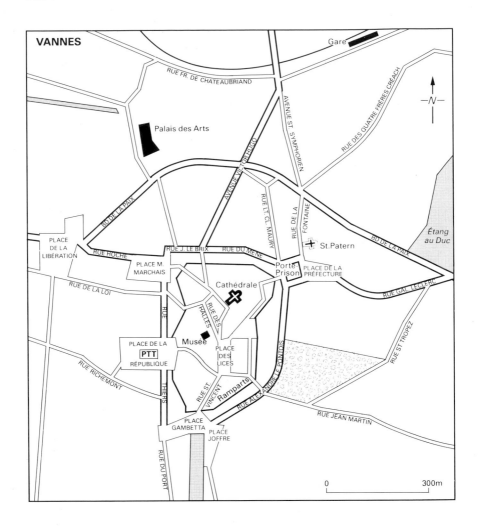

VANNES

Gare

RUE FR. DE CHATEAUBRIAND

Palais des Arts

AVENUE ST. SYMPHORIEN

RUE DES QUATRE FRERES CREACH

—N—

AVENUE DU CTE. HELIUCO

BD DE LA PAIX

PLACE
DE LA
LIBÉRATION

RUE HOCHE

RUE J. LE BRIX

RUE DU MENE

RUE LT.-CL. MAURY

RUE DE LA FONTAINE

St.Patern

BD DE LA PAIX

Étang
au Duc

PLACE M.
MARCHAIS

Porte
Prison

PLACE DE LA
PRÉFECTURE

RUE DE LA LOI

Cathédrale

RUE GAL. LECLERC

RUE DES

RUE ST. TROPEZ

RUE

RUE DES HALLES

Musée

PLACE
DES
LICES

PLACE DE LA
PTT
RÉPUBLIQUE

RUE RICHEMONT

THIERS

RUE ST. VINCENT

Ramparts

RUE ALEXANDRE LE PONTOIS

RUE JEAN MARTIN

PLACE
GAMBETTA

PLACE
JOFFRE

RUE DU PORT

0   300m

century timber-framed wash houses which even today are still used by the more conservative townsfolk.

A narrow street climbs steeply from the Postern Gate to the cathedral, which was six centuries in the building and includes a variety of architecture ranging from Romanesque to Renaissance. It contains the tomb and relics of the town's patron, St. Vincent, who came in fact from Valencia in Spain. He received a ducal summons to Brittany in 1416 after a lifetime of preaching throughout Europe which established him as the great missionary of his age. Unfortunately, after less than three years of evangelism in Brittany he fell ill and died at Vannes, while a great number of white butterflies fluttered at his window, leaving only when he had given up his spirit. The devout took this to be a flight of angels in disguise.

Despite the shortness of his stay among them, St. Vincent made a profound impression on the Breton folk.

There is ample parking in the place des Lices, off rue Thiers, the wide main thoroughfare to the west of the old town, and at the port. The town's main museum, with archaeological finds from many parts of Morbihan, is in a 15th-century house in rue Noë. The tourist office at the southern end of rue Thiers is only too willing to supply brochures and guidance. It also houses a fascinating 'oyster museum'.

There are two main routes west from Vannes to Auray, the major N165 or the lesser D101 which follows as near as is possible the jagged coast, either of which is preferable to the dark, deserted track along which Benjamin Franklin

jolted in a miserable carriage with tired horses on his way to Vannes in 1778. Seven kilometres west of Vannes, the **Pointe d'Arradon** commands extensive views of the gulf and its islands with a comfortable hotel, Les Vénètes, conveniently to hand. Just south of **Baden**, the village of **Larmor-Baden** on a peninsula jutting out into the gulf from the Pen-en-Toul marshes, is the place to embark for the island of **Gavrinis**, site of one of the largest megaliths. Its main chamber covered with a single giant stone lies buried beneath the rocks and turf of a tumulus, the tomb of someone whose fame and power vanished thousands of years ago. The crossing takes 15 minutes.

The road from Baden to Auray crosses a high bridge over the estuary at **Bono**, its little harbour full of fishing

Used even today, the timber-framed wash houses at Vannes date from the 16th century

Menhirs and Dolmens

'*Soyez les bienvenus au pays de menhirs*'—the phrase welcomes visitors to Brittany's outstanding tourist attraction—the stones erected by a mysterious megalithic civilisation. Nowhere in the province are these memorials more extensive than at **Carnac** on the south coast. The name Carnac evokes the British word 'cairn' and Kermario, the Breton name of one of the main alignments means 'village of death'. There are two types of stones—the single standing *menhir* (*men*: stone; *hir*: long) and two uprights supporting a horizontal slab, the *dolmen* (*dol*: table; *men*: stone). Dolmens were burial chambers and were covered with soil to form burial mounds or *tumuli*. Their uncovered remains are to be found all over Europe.

What makes Carnac the prehistoric capital of the world is the staggering number of menhirs and their positioning. The celebrated *alignements* are up to a kilometre or more in length and up to 140 metres wide, running east-north-east across the open heath behind the beach. Nearby are the dolmens of **Kercado**. In July and August the area is thronged with visitors and the narrow roads around it jammed with traffic—it is much better viewed at a quieter time of year.

No one really knows who erected these stones, or why. The latest favourite theory is that they were a sort of Megalithic Jodrell Bank, designed to chart the position of the moon in relation to the stars. The theory goes that this information was important to some long vanished tribe in establishing a calendar for the farming and fishing on which their survival depended. No doubt the stones had spiritual significance for the Druids and their sacrificial rites based on the solstice, but this may have come later.

boats and yachts attracted to this nautical hideaway, and soon afterwards there is a sharp left turning to St. Goustan, where a plaque on a house by the quay commemorates the landing of Benjamin Franklin on his way to Nantes and Paris to solicit aid for the American revolutionaries. A medieval bridge crosses the river to the old town of **Auray** on the opposite bank and a cobbled street climbs the hill to the church and marketplace. There is an even better view from the train as it crosses the viaduct. A piece of ancient Brittany

captured in a loop of the river, Auray defies the traveller to rush through without stopping to stare. It isn't surprising that it is favoured by a school of contemporary artists who hold summer exhibitions here. Despite its sleepy appearance, the town has witnessed some bloody scenes. A little way to the north are a tree-shaded green known as the Champ des Martyrs where 952 royalists were executed by the new republicans in 1795 and the battlefield where, four centuries earlier, Jean de Montfort brought the Breton Wars of Succession to a conclusion in his favour. The road leads on inland to **Ste. Anne-d'Auray**, scene of one of Brit-

Previous page: Half-timbered houses are a feature of Vannes

Other theories: the stones were transported here on the backs of the Korred, elves less than 1m tall with goats' hooves instead of feet; they were laid out in the shape of the Python worshipped at Delphi; they were giant tentpegs in the camp of Caesar's Legion. There is a small museum containing primitive tools and pottery, bones and stone carvings and this, too, becomes excessively crowded in high season. Carnac may be 'the prehistoric capital of the world' but it is by no means the only part of Brittany with an inheritance of megalithic monuments—indeed, they are to be found all over the province.

The immediate area around the Gulf of Morbihan is richly endowed—the **Table des Marchands** near Locmariaquer has a capstone measuring 6m by 4m and the **Grand Menir Brise** originally stood 20m high, although it is now in four pieces. **Roche-aux-Fées** (Fairies' Rock) near Guerche-de-Bretagne is one of the largest megalithic structures in Brittany, 42 stones, some weighing 40 tonnes, guarding a cavernous stone chamber. Its purpose is lost in the mists of time, but courting couples traditionally come here at the time of the new moon and walk around the stones in opposite directions, counting as they go. If, when they meet, their numbers tally they believe their wedding will have 'the blessing of the fairies'. **Les Demoiselles de Langon**, a series of Druids' stones, stand guard on the open moor near Langon (Ille-et-Vilaine) and **Gargantua's Finger** is a standing stone at the approach to the fortress of La Latte (Côtes-du-Nord, west of St. Malo). More unexpectedly, on a green island amongst the tarmac in the residential suburbs of the shipbuilding town of St. Nazaire, stands a dolmen with two uprights and a capstone and beside it a solitary menhir pointing at the sky.

tany's most celebrated *pardons*. It honours a statue of the mother of the Virgin Mary which was discovered buried in the earth by a local farmer in 1623. A 19th-century basilica and a huge memorial to Bretons who died in World War I dominate the great open space where thousands gather at the end of July.

The road south on the western shore of the River d' Auray heads around the coast to Carnac. Just beyond Crac'h is a road signposted to **Locmariaquer**, and lined with cottages selling oysters, mussels and other shellfish, tastings invited. Locmariaquer is a pretty little port full of

crêperies, shops selling *articles de pêche* and comfortable small hotels, grouped around a church with a slate-clad spire. There is a children's carousel on the quay where *vedettes panoramiques* takes on passengers for trips around the islands. This little peninsula is megalith country. The Grand Menhir and the Table des Marchands lie just off the road to Locmariaquer and beyond the town the tumulus Mane er Hroech lies half hidden amid ferns and gorse. A dark stone-lined tunnel leads underground down a flight of steps plunging into a thicket of brambles. From above there's a view of the wide blue waters of the Gulf dotted with white sails. The

Pierres Plates dolmen stand at the edge of the beach and seaweed-covered rocks exposed at low tide when people with rakes and buckets hunt for shellfish. A lonely campsite stands among the pine trees. The road ends at the pointe de Kerpenhir, where a redundant World War II German gun emplacement still stands guard, its mountings slowly rusting away, beside a statue of the Virgin and child. Opposite lies Port-Navlo and the narrow neck of the Gulf of Morbihan through which a steady stream of yachts, fishing boats and cruising vessels beat their way. The 'Little Sea' and its wooded islands offer countless possibilities to the cruising yacht and the 'passeport Morbihan' provides, for an annual fee, overnight berths and use of toilet facilities ashore in eight harbours, Port-Haliguen, Port-Crouesty, Port-Blanc, Île aux Moines, Arradon, Arzal Camoel, La Roche-Bernard and La Trinité-sur-Mer (tel 97.42.63.44).

La Trinité-sur-Mer, going west on the D781 over the high bridge which gives sweeping views of the Crac'h estuary, is the Cowes of France, its jetties lined with million dollar yachts where 25 years ago there was nothing but rotting hulks amid hectares of oyster beds. Now the boutiques, chandleries and crêperies along the quay are crowded in summer. An inviting *pension* in a flower-filled garden, Les Hortensias, stands apart on the hillside, looking down on this bustling scene. The port faces the wide waters of Quiberon Bay, sheltered by the long peninsula on its western side and two islands, Houat and Hoedic, both with golden beaches away from the crowds, idyllic

Megaliths like these make Carnac the prehistoric capital

93

for windsurfing and swimming. If La Trinité is the French equivalent of Cowes,
then Quiberon Bay is its Solent, used by
racing yacht's for tuning and training.

Carnac-Plage, west of La Trinité, has a
splendid long sandy beach backed by
dunes and pinewoods, large enough
never to be uncomfortably crowded
even though the woods are full of campsites, caravans, chalets, *gîtes*, *pensions*,
hotels and every other conceivable type
of holiday accommodation. The caravans Eurocamp style are far removed
from the primitive chalet that we knew
on our first family holiday here, with
showers, flush toilets, and space to
relax in. Even the tents are an improvement on that chalet. The town of
Carnac behind the beach has many
shops and hotels, the largest of which is
the 110-bed Novotel Tal Ar Mor in the
avenue Atlantique.

Carnac has more to offer than seaside pleasures, acceptable though they
are in fine weather. It is as if Stonehenge
was picked up and deposited on the
Dorset coast. One kilometre or so from
the buckets and spades and ice cream
cornets, spread along route D196 are
ten rows of megaliths, sprouting from
the moorland turf like white sabre teeth.
It is claimed, should you wish to verify
it, that they number precisely 1,099 but
no one knows who put them there (see
Box). It is worth visiting the museum in
the town to find out what precisely is
known and to see further finds from the
prehistoric sites, although it must be
said that it becomes excessively
crowded in high season. Tours inside
the Tumulus de St. Michel are conducted by candlelight. Another sight
not to be missed is the 17th-century
church of St. Cornély, the patron saint
of farm animals and of Carnac, where a

cattle festival is held in his honour every
13 September. He was an early pope,
martyred under Emperor Decius, who is
said to have fled Rome in a chariot
drawn by two oxen. The pagan army
pursued him north through Italy and
westwards through Gaul until they
reached Carnac, where he turned upon
them with a curse so powerful that it
transfigured the ranks of soldiers into
stone, and they are standing there in
that state of petrification to this day. If
this seems one of the more unlikely
explanations of the *alignements* of Carnac it is none the less amusing to see
among the curious paintings on the
wooden vault inside the church a relief
of St. Cornély smiling inscrutably between a pair of oxen.

From Carnac and the main coast road
(D781) route D768 runs southwards
along a strip of land not much wider
than the road itself (in places no more
than 7 metres during high spring tides)
with the sea on both sides. Its shape has
been compared to a stranded frigate. At
its tip the peninsula swells out around
the port of **Quiberon**, 15km from Carnac. The Presqu'île de Quiberon is an
outing in itself, with its wild Atlantic
shore (Côte Sauvage) traversed by a dramatic corniche and its sheltered eastern
coast of tranquil harbours and the vistas
of the Sables Blancs behind the pines
and the dunes. There are numerous
hotels (including the 120-bed Sofitel) at
Quiberon and Port-Haliguen, St. Pierre
and St. Julien, all within 7km of each
other. The main harbour provides
plenty of shipping activity to watch.

Ferries sail from here to **Belle-Île**, the
most romantic of Breton islands, a place
of grottoes and wheeling seabirds, with
a palace and the fort that was actress
Sarah Bernhardt's summer retreat and is

now the clubhouse of the newest addition to the island's amenities, an 18-hole golf course. The crossing to the main port of Le Palais, a lively town, takes 45 minutes. The island is about 15km long and between 5km and 10km wide, so it is useful to take a car (a booking on the ferry is essential) but more fun to hire a bicycle. At weekends the crowds from the mainland flock there. Sauzon, on the eastern more sheltered side of the island just a few kilometres north of Le Palais, is quieter, remarkably like a little Cornish town nestled among its cliffs and sandy coves. There are several quiet and secluded hotels for those wanting a longer sojourn and a good restaurant La Forge at Bangor. Belle-Île is a favourite port of call for cruising boats, with special mooring buoys for them at Le Palais and berths in the harbour and marina at Sauzon.

Quiberon to Quimperlé

Between the Presqu'île de Quiberon and the Lorient estuary the coast is less jagged, with long straight beaches and expanses of dunes. It is easy to pass straight through **Erdeven**, a village of grey stone (even its church steeple) without a second glance. That could be a mistake. The alignements at **Kerzerho** lie a kilometre to the south-east on a by-road and the notable dolmen of Crucuno is 3km beyond. Apart from these antiquities Erdeven is well placed for a health and fitness holiday with the thalassotherapy centre at nearby Carnac and an excellent 18-hole public golf course at Ploemel, 3km away. Erdeven also has good places at which to lunch

or dine in style at reasonable prices: the Voyageurs on rue de l'Océan, the Hubert opposite the church and the Auberge du Sous-Bois, a kilometre along the route Pont-Lorois. Inexpensive rooms are available. More expensive, but good value, the 18th-century Château de Kéravéon stands in its own park 1.5km away on the D105. It's intriguing to note how many names have the prefix 'Ker' which is simply Breton for 'place'. Travelling west, the towns and villages become more distinctively Breton and road signs are printed in that language as well as French. Older men wear berets and women in white lace coiffes are seen, although not as frequently as they were even a few years ago.

The estuary at **Etel** opens out into the great lake or lagoon of the rivière and there are impressive views of it from the D781 which crosses it over a suspension bridge before going on to **Port-Louis**, a fairly quiet fishing port and small resort. It has a granite-walled 17th-century citadel and two museums, one devoted to the Compagnie des Indes and the other to the Arsenal set up by Louis XIII, the port's founder. **Lorient**, the naval base and dockyard across the estuary, took over from Port-Louis as the home port of the French equivalent of the East India Company in 1666 and was named accordingly. Alas, there is little romance about it today other than its name. During World War II it was an important base for U-boat hunter-killer packs and was virtually razed during the Allied liberation of 1944 when the Germans held out there as they did at St. Malo, Brest and St. Nazaire (some of the heavily fortified submarine pens which survived are open to visitors). Lorient has a magnificent location at the mouth of the

The purpose of the standing stones at Kerzerho remains a mystery

River Scorff where it joins up with the Blavet and it is almost worth taking the train from Auray to get a view of this estuary from the viaduct as you enter the city. In August it is the scene of a festival which attracts 4,500 musicians, dancers, singers, composers and writers in the Celtic tradition, including many from Britain and Ireland. The Festival Interceltique de Lorient was started 20 years ago and is now an established event in the Brittany festival calendar.

Northwards from Port-Louis route D781 hugs the east bank of the wide River Blavet to **Hennebont**, which seems entangled in a knot of major

Calm water in Port-Haliguen at the tip of the Quiberon peninsula

routes all converging and entwining here. All that survives of ancient Hennebont is a few stones of the town walls and the restored Porte du Broerch, alongside the church of Notre-Dame-du-Paradis, which dates from the 16th century and has a notable steeple and belfry. Four kilometres south of Hennebont on route D781, the gorgeous Château de Locguénolé stands in a sunny park overlooking the river which an English fleet navigated to rescue Jeanne de la Flamme. It incorporates the Résidence de Kernavien and its cooking rates two Michelin stars, benefiting no doubt from the fact that the famous fish auctions of Lorient are only just across the estuary by boat or 14km by road.

Sorting fish for the criée, or auction, at Lorient

Skirting the city of Lorient, route N165 heads across country to Quimperlé, passing the airport of Lann-Bihoué, only an hour from Paris by regular scheduled services. A pretty road (D152) runs around the coast from Lar-mor-Plage south of Lorient to **Guidel-Plages** where L'Auberge Cadieu offers 18 pleasant, bright rooms with facilities. Its restaurant, overlooking the beach and the estuary of the River Laita, is busy with families, serving good food at very reasonable prices. Just across the river mouth which marks the boundary of Morbihan and Finistère is the little port of **Le Pouldu** where Gauguin 'walked about like a savage and did nothing at all' (see page 102), today a quiet and charming little resort with two nice family hotels, Armen and Bains. A statue of the painter stands near the church. From the main beach there's a

splendid view of the Île de Groix. The route from Guidel-Plages to Le Pouldu is a somewhat roundabout one although by boat it's a matter of minutes.

Quimperlé is situated about 15km inland at the point where the rivers Ellé and Isole merge to form the Laita. Roads approach the town from the south on either side of the Laita but the loveliest route from the coast is that through the forest of Carnoët, one of the few remaining traces of the woodlands that once covered the interior of Brittany. Quimperlé is an attractive place of tree-shaded squares and cobbled streets, a town for browsing around or shopping. Its name, like that of Quimper, comes from the Breton word 'kemper' or confluence of rivers. The river in question, the Ellé, tumbles boisterously under a stone bridge in the Ville Basse while the Isole rushes under another as if they can't wait to get together.

This part of town is dominated by the circular basilica of the Église Ste. Croix which stands on a sort of island between the two rivers and is modelled on the church of the Holy Sepulchre in Jerusalem. It predates the Gothic style with its rounded Romanesque apses, tower and even roofs. A Renaissance screen glorifies Christ and the four Evangelists, amid a lacework of carving and figures. Medieval houses with projecting upper storeys stand in the shadow of this distinctive church. The hill which rises from the opposite bank of the Isole is crowned by Quimperlé's other main church, the more traditional Gothic Notre Dame de l'Assomption. Its interior is of stark simplicity with a calvary in stained glass above the altar. The steeply inclined rue Savary, paved and decorated with flowers in wood boxes, some incorporating seats, is for pedestrians only and has many attractive shops, selling shoes and fashions as well as souvenirs. La Maison du Blanc at number 33 (tel 98.96.02.87) specialises in lace.

Cornouaille, the Breton Cornwall, has no official boundaries or precise definition but it begins, if anywhere, here at Quimperlé, although its main town is Quimper. In wry acknowledgement of this, local people say that if Quimper is the smile of Cornouaille, then Quimperlé 'is its kiss'.

Quimperlé to Quimper

This is the Côte de Cornouaille; an area that combines all that is most attractive about holidays in Brittany: crêpes and cider, oysters and mussels, calvaries and watermills, dolmens and menhirs, boules and pétanque, *pardons* and Celtic folk festivals, sailing, boating, fishing, rambling, tennis, and of course beautiful beaches. The Pays de L'Aven-Bélon immediately to the west of the Laita estuary is just over 500km from Paris (120km of which is motorway) or an hour by air to Lorient, Quimper or Brest. Doëlan, a tiny port on an inlet from the sea, is noted for the cider that comes from the orchards round about. Just to the north, **Moëlan-sur-Mer**, a quiet little town with a small fish market and a 15th-century calvary beside the grey stone church of St. Philibert, is actually a little way inland from the sandy beaches with rocks that shimmer gold in the sunshine and secretive creeks of Bélon, Brigneau and Merrien. It's said to take its name from Irish monk Moë

who built his hermitage ('lan' in Breton) here, but an alternative theory is that it was a sacred site during the Roman period, Medislanum. Certainly, its roots go back into prehistory, evidenced by the dolmens, menhirs and tombs scattered about the surrounding countryside. Tiny hamlets are built around common plots, sheltered from the Atlantic winds by screens of elms and there is a 15th-century pigeon loft at Kermoguer. A garrison house with a granite roof guards the mouth of Merrien harbour alongside the lighthouse and the heath and woodland round about is under the permanent protection of the Conservatoire Naturel de l'Espace Littoral. Guided walks of two to three hours are arranged from the tourist office in Moëlan (rue des Moulins, tel 98.39.67.28).

Native Bélon oysters, excellent farmhouse cider and charcuterie are the gastronomic specialities here. Wooded valleys and paths run down to the rivers Bélon and Aven. There is a 9km coastal walk through landscape designated as a national area of exceptional beauty to the ruined fort, built to guard the double estuary of the two rivers. The Rosbras Sailing Centre on the banks of the Aven is one of the most important in France and many champions have learned to sail here. There are courses on cruisers, sailboards and dinghies with a fleet of Optimists for the 9-14 year olds (detailed information from the Syndicat d'Intiative in place de l'Église, tel 98.06.97.65). West of the estuary run 15km of usually almost deserted sands, with small inlets where boats are drawn up, blending into heath and open fields with occasional low sandy cliffs and outcrops of rock. Port-Manech, Kerdruc, Rospico, Kerascoët, Raguenès are the place names that evoke the magic of

this symphony of unspoiled land and sea, a camping, fishing and boating haven. There are many well-appointed campsites and safe anchorages.

Pont-Aven stands at the head of the estuary, a market town that used to have almost as many watermills as houses. Cambry, an 18th-century travel writer, described it thus: 'It stands on the water on rocks at the front of two high hills, on which are strewn enormous rounded blocks of granite which seem about to topple over; they serve as gables for thatched cottages or as walls for small gardens. Watermills standing on the river bank use them to support the axles of their water wheels; wooden bridges link them together...The noise of the river, the roar of twenty waterfalls deafen the traveller, as did the fulling mills in Don Quixote, or like the waterfalls in Switzerland or in Savoy.' It was this peculiar charm which captivated writers, poets and painters from Gauguin down. Many of the ancient watermills and houses survive and it would be difficult to imagine a more 'paintable' or photogenic place. In 1905 the songwriter and poet Théodore Botrel set up the first folklore festival in Brittany in the shade of the Bois d'Amour here. He called it the Gorse Flower Festival (Fleurs d'Ajoncs) and it is still held, on the first Sunday in August, every year, providing an opportunity to see traditional Breton dances and the colourful local costume including the distinctive *coiffe* or bonnet of starched linen and lace worn by the women. Pont-Aven is famous, too, for its biscuits and butter cake (kouign-amann), its cider and mead (chouchen) and the sardine and tuna which comes from its canneries.

A museum in the place de l'Hôtel-de-Ville devoted to the life and works of the Pont-Aven School headed by Gauguin and including Emile Bernard, Serusier, Maufra, Filiger, Moret and others attracts 25,000 visitors a year. The town these days has as many art galleries as it once had watermills, as well as a disco and nightclubs. Some of the ancient mills and houses on the banks of the Aven survive and one of them is now the restaurant le Moulin de Rosmadec, with a terrace overlooking the river, beamed ceiling, traditional Breton furniture and gleaming brass ornaments. The food lives up to the surroundings which means, alas, that in season there is rarely a table to spare.

An alternative if you are headed for Concarneau is La Taupinière (4km on route D783) where cider and seafood is blended to magical effect. **Concarneau** is known more for its fish auctions and its annual Fête des Filets Bleus (festival of the Blue Nets) at the end of August than for its folk festival which takes place a month earlier. Viewed from the bridge which carries the main road past the town, the new harbour is crammed with oceangoing fishing boats. It remains the third biggest fishing port in France with a large tunny fleet; it even has a museum in rue Vauban devoted to fishing, with some of the earliest sardine tins on view. It would be unthinkable to visit Concarneau without sampling the local fish soup and it seems to be a speciality of any restaurant one cares to go into.

The old walled town or Ville Close occupies an island in the middle of the old harbour, separating the inner port

Opposite: The back streets of Quimperlé are irresistible

101

Paul Gauguin (1848–1903)

Among the most famous paintings of this celebrated artist is *Le Christe Jaune* ('The Yellow Christ') and the inspiration for it can be seen in the little chapel of Trémalo in the wooded hills above Pont-Aven: a wood figure of Christ on the cross. Gauguin first went to Pont-Aven in 1886, a few years after giving up an office job in Paris to become a full-time painter, and settled for a time in Brittany where he became the leading light in the art movement known as Synthesism. Pont-Aven was a town of windmills full of people in Breton costume prepared to sit as models. Artists from the Latin Quarter in Paris migrated there for a summer to paint, play cards and drink at the Pension Gloanec.

While living at Pont-Aven, Gauguin offered *The Vision after the Sermon* (now in the National Gallery of Scotland) free to the priest of a nearby village. His offer was turned down on the grounds that the locals wouldn't 'understand' the painting. The motto of the Gauguin school was 'Paint what you see, not what is there'.

In 1889 Gauguin moved to the even quieter village of Le Pouldu at the mouth of the River Laïta where, in his own words, he 'walked about like a savage and did nothing at all'. All the same, he made long trips abroad to Martinique and Tahiti and spent some time with Van Gogh at Arles after which the latter cut off his own ear with a razor. Gauguin was involved in a brawl in Concarneau after children taunted his mistress 'Anna the Javanese', who went around with a tame monkey on her shoulder. Sailors drinking at a café joined in and kicked Gauguin with their sabots after he had suffered a broken leg. Gauguin left Brittany and Europe in 1895 to spend his last years in the remote South Seas colonies of France, dying in poverty, ravaged by syphilis, and leaving on his easel the painting *A Breton Village Under Snow* which is now in the Louvre.

from the outer which is packed with expensive yachts. The marina was devastated by the hurricane of October 1987 but is now fully restored. The Ville Close is reached by bridges from the quayside and within its ramparts, started in the 14th century and completed 300 years later by Vauban (noted for his military architecture throughout Brittany, and indeed France), there is a maze of alleys and courts, squares and steps. There is no escape, however, from fish: either the all-pervading smell of it or the view through archways and around every corner of nets and boats.

A pathway runs around the top of the ramparts and provides a good vantage point for watching the ships putting out to sea. A hydrojet service operates daily in summer from the marina to the isles of Glénan, home of the famous sailing school, in 25 minutes.

If you are headed for the Pointe du Cabellou, a favourite local beach resort, from the direction of Quimperlé make a left turning *before* you get to the Moros bridge at Concarneau. North of the town is a long stretch of fine sand Les Sables Blancs with open views across the lovely Baie de la Forêt. M.

The Ville Close or walled town occupies an island in the middle of the old harbour at Concarneau

and Mme. Henaff, who run the well-established Hôtel de la Baie at **La Forêt-Fouesnant**, in 1988 opened their new Hôtel de l'Océan, in this pleasant setting. It is an enjoyable drive on major roads around the bay to La Forêt, which used to be a little visited hamlet, standing at the head of one of the creeks which are left almost high and dry when the tide flows out into the bay. There is a pleasant walk along the banks of the River St. Laurent opening into a fjord-like estuary, especially on a calm evening when the trees are reflected on the mirror surface of the water. Freshwater and sea fishing enthusiasts find good sport here. The building of Port-la-Forêt, a vast marina for all kinds of leisure craft in 1972, with 550 permanent moorings, has brought much tourist activity to the area but the village clustered around an interesting 16th-century church with the descriptive

name of Our Lady of the Low Sea of the Bay remains typically Breton. It has an ancient calvary, a fine slender steeple, bells cast in 1614 and many curious statues inside, eleven of them carved from wood. It is surrounded by woods and orchards yet Kerleven beach with its club for young children is only a couple of kilometres away. At the end of a private drive off route D783, 1.5km north of the village is the 16th-century Manoir du Stang, one of the first old châteaux to be converted into a hotel more than 50 years ago. Apart from the beauty of the house itself with its wood panelling and period furniture, the grounds with their beautiful displays of flowers, lakes and woods, are utterly peaceful.

Overleaf: Concarneau is famous for its criée (fish auction)

Bénodet is a mecca for British as well as French yachting enthusiasts

The village of **Fouesnant**, 3km west, is surrounded by apple and cherry orchards. Some of the best (if not *the* best) and certainly most potent cider in Brittany is produced here, although oddly enough in July a beer festival at the Halles des Sports is widely promoted. More advertised in fact, than the Pardon of Ste. Anne, which takes place at the same time in and around a country church to the north of the village and brings out the particularly beautiful local costumes. Route D45 heads south from Fouesnant to **Beg-Meil,** 5.5km away, a former fishing village with a string of coves fringed with white sand and pines, divided by rocky outcrops full of little pools. In high season English is heard more than any other tongue, including French. Red and blue lobster boats unload their catches at the jetty,

which also serves as a departure point for pleasure boats. The *Jeanne Yvonne* shuttles back and forth across the beautiful Baie de la Forêt to Concarneau (a 30-minute trip costing 15F each way). The *Perle de Beg Meil* cruises up the River Odet to Quimper and to the fascinating, low-lying **Îles des Glénan** which can be seen on the horizon far out to sea, yet only 90 minutes away by motorboat or a morning's sailing. They comprise hundreds of outcrops, teeming with birdlife, with crystal clear lagoons and dazzling white beaches. Some are uninhabited, perfect for picnics and barbecues.

Between Beg-Meil and the Pointe de Mousterlin to the west there is little but sand, rocks and solitude, reached by narrow unnumbered lanes, the ideal place to get away from it all, although only 6km from Fouesnant. At the mouth of the River Odet is **Bénodet** which over the years has become a mecca for British as well as French yachting folk. The cast of the British television soap *Howard's Way* would fit in instantly here. The tide runs strongly through the inlet but there are plenty of moorings and a marina on the eastern bank. Ashore, the accommodation remains in small family-run hotels. Although camping sites are numerous hereabouts, Bénodet somehow manages to retain a bit of snob appeal. There is a casino and nightlife of sorts. A fine golfing complex has been developed around a new 18-hole course at **Clohars Foesnant**, 4km away. Bénodet manages to keep its Brittany flavour and the market stalls sell locally made lace. Boat services run to the Glénan Isles and upriver to Quimper, 16km between steep wooded banks graced with the châteaux of well-heeled Parisiennes.

The Odet, with its tributaries and inlets, widening in places to the dimensions of a lake, is made for day excursions and, unusually in this age of pollution, the water is remarkably clean and clear.

The Southern Argoat

Having traversed the coast from Vannes to Quimper, it would be wrong to disregard the rest of the southern part of Basse Bretagne which lies inland, the Argoat or mythical 'land of the woods'. We have already ventured into it going west from Rennes to Ploërmel and Josselin (Chapter 5). The river-cum-canal which flows at the foot of Josselin's spectacular battlements continues north-westwards before looping south-westerly to **Pontivy** where it meets the River Blavet, flowing down to the sea at Lorient. Pontivy is an important market town with a moated castle built in the 15th century by the Rohan family but by Breton standards it is somewhat parvenu as it was founded not by the saints of old but by someone as recent as Napoleon Bonaparte. Perhaps seeing its central position as useful in keeping this troublesome province under control, he established a garrison, law courts, town hall and lycée here. There are some ancient houses in the rues du Fil, du Pont and du Dr-Guépin, around the church of Notre-Dame-de-la-Joie, but most of the streets and avenues flanking the Blavet run as straight as a line of soldiers, to a meticulous grid pattern, and one of the grand avenues is named after Napoleon. Indeed, for a brief spell after the Revolution the whole town was named after him.

Napoleonville. It became, too, a half-way port for the commercial traffic on the Canal de Nantes à Brest. These days only pleasure craft use the canal but there is considerable activity at the locks in summer.

South of Pontivy, it pays to leave the main D768 to explore the network of attractive, quiet country roads which lie to the west of the River Blavet and pass through villages and hamlets of great charm; places such as St. Nicholas-des-Eaux, St. Nicodème, Melrand and Bieuzy. The Site de Castennec, around which Route D1 and the Blavet wind lasso-like, owes it fame to the legend that St. Gildas lived in a cave there. The 16th-century chapel at Quelven contains a statue of the Virgin which opens to show twelve carvings of scenes from the life of Christ, which is at the centre of the annual *pardon* on 15 August. Whichever road you take is likely to lead you to scenes of myth and legend. Above a fountain outside **Baud** stands a larger than life, almost naked stone female figure, of apparently ancient origin. It is marked on the Michelin road map with a little triangle and the words

Pontivy's moated castle was built by the Rohans in the 15th century

Vénus de Quinipily but it isn't that easy to find. It is worth making the effort, though, because of the mystery attached to this rather ungainly Goddess of Love. Is she Egyptian, Roman, an idol of the ancient Gauls, or merely a fake? As with the menhirs and dolmens, no one really knows, but this *Ar Gwreg Houarn* (Iron Woman), as the Breton peasantry called her, once stood on a hill near Castennec. The powers of the church resented the reverence that was shown to her and had her thrown in the River Blavet but each time she was recovered. One story says that St. Gildas buried her in his cave. The existing Vénus is almost certainly a late 17th-century copy named after the Seigneur de Quinipily who ordered it.

Travelling west from Pontivy, one arrives at the upper reaches of the Scorff, the river which meets up with the Blavet at Lorient. Guémené-sur-Scorff has very little left of its once impregnable castle walls; the ravages of time have seen to that. **Kernascléden**, a small village a few kilometres downriver, is more interesting because of the frescoes inside its 16th-century church, presenting a glimpse of hell calculated to keep the faithful firmly on the straight and narrow path. **Le Faouet**, 15km to the west, abounds with religious monuments: the chapels of Ste. Barbe in a hillside niche above the town, St. Nicholas on the road to Priziac and St. Fiacre, near the River Ellé to the south. But even if a round of chapels is not to your taste, the tour is worth it for the unsurpassed loveliness of the countryside.

The ancient calvary of our Lady of the Low Sea of the Bay at Forêt-Fouesnant

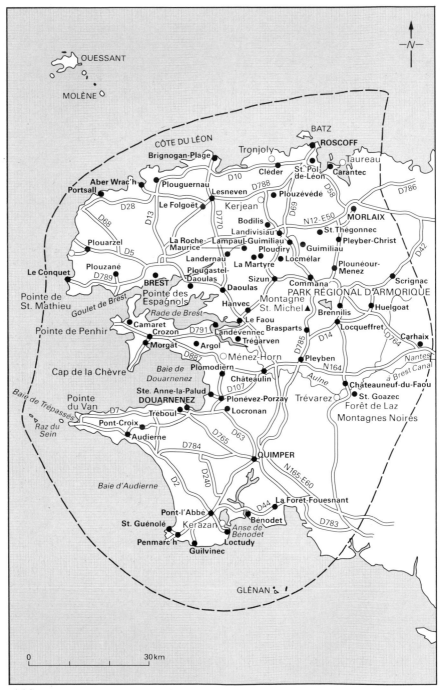

OUESSANT

MOLÈNE

CÔTE DU LÉON

BATZ

Tronjoly

ROSCOFF

Brignogan-Plage

Taureau

Cléder

St. Pol-
de-Léon

Carantec

Aber Wrac'h

Plouguernau

D10

Portsall

Lesneven

D788

Plouzévédé

D786

Le Folgoët

Kerjean

D69

D58

D28

D13

Bodilis

MORLAIX

D770

Landivisiau

N12-E50

St. Thégonnec

Plouarzel

La Roche-
Maurice

Lampaul-Guimiliau

Pleyber-Christ

Ploudiry

Guimiliau

D42

Landernau

Locmélar

Plounéour-
Menez

Plouzané

Plougastel-
Daoulas

La Martyre

Scrignac

Le Conquet

D789

BREST

Sizun

Commana

PARK RÉGIONAL D'ARMORIQUE

Pointe de
St. Mathieu

Pointe des
Espagnols

Daoulas

Montagne
St. Michel ▲

Huelgoat

Goulet de Brest

Rade de Brest

Hanvec

Brennilis

Pointe de Penhir

Camaret

Le Faou

Locqueffret

D764

Carhaix

Crozon

D791

Brasparts

D785

D14

Landevennec

Argol

Trégarven

Nantes

Morgat

D887

Ménez-Horn

Pleyben

à Brest Canal

Cap de la Chèvre

Baie de
Douarnenez

Plomodiern

N164

Aulne

Châteaulin

Pointe
du Van

Ste. Anne-la-Palud

D107

Plonévez-Porzay

Trévarez

Châteauneuf-du-Faou

St. Goazec

DOUARNENEZ

Baie de Trépassés

Trébourl

Locronan

Forêt de Laz
Montagnes Noires

Raz du
Sein

Pont-Croix

D7

Audierne

D765

D63

Baie d'Audierne

D784

QUIMPER

D2

D240

N165-E60

La Forêt-Fouesnant

Pont-l'Abbé

D44

St. Guénolé

Kérazan

Bénodet

D783

Penmarc'h

Anse de
Bénodet

Loctudy

Guilvinec

GLÉNAN

0   30km

110

7
From Quimper to the Côte du Léon

Quimper

Like Quimperlé, **Quimper** derives its name from a Frenchified spelling of the Breton word 'kemper', meaning a confluence of rivers, in this case three, the Odet and the Steir and the gentle Jet. Not only is Quimper the prefecture of the *département* of Finistère, it is an unofficial capital, too, of that much older region known as Cornouaille, echoing Cornwall from whence so many of the Celtic migrants to Brittany came. Cornouaille simply doesn't exist on any map but its ancient writ runs from Quimperlé to the Bay of Douarnenez and around the jagged south-west coast of Brittany, including its equivalent of Land's End, the Pointe du Raz. Quimper is the most Breton of Breton cities, poles apart from the much larger regional capital of Rennes and putting Brest, the big brother of Finistère, completely in the shade as far as tourism is concerned. It is 553km from Paris, or just an hour via the Quimper-Pluguffan airport to the west of the town. Since 1989 when the Atlantic TGV service was introduced as far as Rennes, the journey by train to Quimper from Paris Montparnasse has been reduced from over five hours to 4 hours 21 minutes. Its relative isolation made Quimper the

Siberia of 17th-century France—Louis XIII banished his confessor there when he was caught plotting against Cardinal Richelieu. To this day, its inhabitants complain—only half jokingly—that they are 'the forgotten French'.

Quimper is an untidy, bustling, old-fashioned country town where crêpes and cider are the staff of life, where women wearing sabots and shawls are part of the everyday scene, not merely prettied up in gowns and *coiffes* for folk-lore festivals. Blue is Quimper's colour and the Breton name for a Quimperoise is Glazik, 'little blue'. Every year, towards the end of July, the town abandons itself totally to the biggest folk festival of all, the Fêtes de Cornouaille. Quimper has been host to this celebration since 1923 but from its beginnings of local people in traditional costume, singing and dancing to the music of the *biniou* (bagpipe) and *bombarde* (oboe) it has become an international event with thousands of participants from many countries in their own national costumes. For seven days the tree-lined boulevards and leafy squares with their terrace cafés ring with the music handed down through generations and on the final Sunday a procession through the town—the Grand Défile à Travers la Ville—provides a cultural tour of Brittany in costume, music and dance, around its coast and through the Argoat, beginning and ending at Quimper. Even when not en fête, Quimper is a lively, smiling place, matching the mood of the River Odet which gurgles happily through it over a rocky bed, swallowing up the lesser streams of the Jet and the Steir, which flows through the old town from north to south. On the north bank of the Odet, the Cathedral points two lacy spires at the sky and, a little way west of it, the busy marketplace is surrounded by cobbled streets of half-timbered buildings that look like medieval dolls' houses. The plentiful supply of water and fuel from the surrounding woods, together with deposits of white clay, encouraged the potteries which existed here 2,000 years ago, and continue to prosper

Cobbled streets of half-timbered houses lead to the cathedral at Quimper

today. The distinctive faïences de Quimper are sold everywhere and especially in the rue Keréon which runs from the cathedral to the bridge over the Steir, with its enchanting view of the old town. L'Art du Cornouaille in the cathedral square is a good place to shop for Quimper pottery, or antiques and lace.

The Gothic Cathedral, built between the 13th and 15th centuries although the twin spires were not added until the 19th, is one of the most magnificent in Brittany with some rare examples of 15th-century stained glass and an organ that was reconstructed in 1643 by an Englishman, Robert Dallam, who emigrated to Brittany to escape Puritanism. The cathedral is dedicated to St. Corentin, Quimper's first bishop and its patron saint, who is credited with having fed himself and others indefinitely on one small, but miraculous fish. Each time he cut a piece off it to eat he threw the remainder back into the pool, where it became whole again. Among those who shared a piece of this remarkable fish was King Gradlon, who was so impressed that he rewarded Corentin with the bishopric of the new town of Kemper. King Gradlon was ruler of the city of Ys in the Dark Ages and legend tells how he was betrayed by his daughter Dahut, who fell in love with the Devil. The Devil, in the guise of a young prince, persuaded her to bring him the key to the sluice gates that kept the sea out and which the King kept around his neck at all times. Dahut took the key while he slept and the Devil opened the gates, drowning the city for all time. Gradlon escaped on his horse

Opposite: The lacy spires of Quimper Cathedral

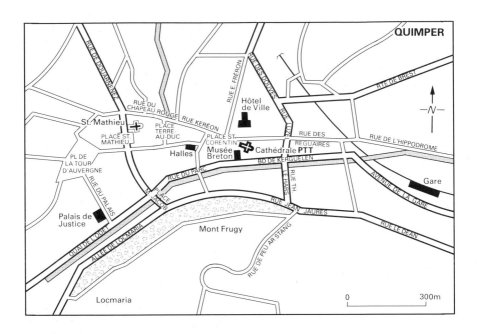

Morvarc'h ('Horse of the Sea'), pushing his daughter back into the waves when she tried to cling on. Today he sits mounted in stone on Morvarc'h between the twin spires of the Cathedral. Next to this building so rich in legend, in the former bishop's palace, is a museum containing more matter-of-fact legacies of pottery and other artefacts. One room is fitted out as any Breton home would have been with *lit-clos* (box-bed), chests, table, benches and cupboards. Another displays a variety of Cornouaille country costume. The Musée des Beaux-Arts on the other side of place Laennec is based on the collection of the Comte de Silguy and contains the works of Italian and Dutch masters as well as Breton artists, pre-Impressionist and Impressionist, and Max Jacob, lifelong friend of Picasso and the best known of Quimperois artists and writers. The main bridge across the Odet is named after Jacob, as

is the small courtyard off the rue du Parc where he was born in 1876 to a family of Jewish shopkeepers. He converted to Catholicism in his thirties and for a time lived a monastic life at St. Benoît-sur-Loire near Orleans. Despite this, during the German occupation of France in World War II he was made to wear the yellow Star of David and died in 1944 at Drancy, a transit camp for Jews on the way to the gas chambers.

Outside the Musée Breton, the close in the shadow of a large weeping willow tree leads through a cloister to a surviving section of the ramparts which used to surround the Ville Close of the Middle Ages. One can promenade here in the footsteps of the bishops looking across the river to Mont Frugy, slopes heavy with beeches rising steeply from the north riverside. The views in the opposite direction from Mont Frugy of the cathedral and the old town are similarly rewarding. The area of the old town west of the River Steir was the Terre au Duc (Duke's Domain) and its streets or vennels (a word still used in the city of Durham in northern England) are quaintly named the Venelle du Pain Cuit, Venelle du Moulin-du-Duc, Venelle du Poivre and so on. The site of the ancient potteries is a short way down the Odet where it widens on its journey to the sea, at Locmaria, which has a striking Romanesque church. When the Romans made pottery here it was called Aquilonia. Quimper ware as it is known today throughout the world is based on 19th-century Grande Maison patterns and the competing houses finally amalgamated in 1968 to form Les Faïenceries de Quimper H.-B. Henriot (tel 98.90.09.36). There are 90-minute conducted tours throughout the week, and a museum of crockery.

Quimper to Douarnenez

To the west of the Odet estuary, spanned by an elegant modern road bridge 610m long, is the *pays* Bigouden, an out-of-the-way and very traditional corner of Brittany where the women still wear a particularly tall (32cm) lace *coiffe* at festivals and *pardons*. A display of them can be seen at other times at the Musée Bigouden in the castle at Pont-l'Abbé. Ste. Marine, facing Bénodet across the narrows, is a quieter (and even prettier) spot with its own small fishing and sailing harbour and a fine sandy beach several kilometres long. It has a Michelin-starred restaurant Le Jeanne d'Arc which does wonderful things with local lobster, fish and artichokes.

Pont-l'Abbé, the Bigouden's capital, got its name from a bridge built by the monks from the abbey at Loctudy, 6km to the south. It sits astride an inlet from the sea and apart from the castle already mentioned built between the 14th and 18th centuries, it has many lovely 17th-century houses, a good shopping centre and an array of fine beaches within easy reach. The road to Loctudy passes the Château de Kerazan, where Joseph Astor endowed a school of embroidery and needlework for local girls in 1929. The manor house is open to visitors and has an interesting collection of paintings and drawings going back four centuries. The little fishing port and seaside resort of Loctudy, typically Cornouaille, faces the peninsula of Île Tudy, stretched like a finger across the mouth of the Pont-l'Abbé river with beaches sloping gently to the sea on either side from sheltering sand dunes.

The pays Bigouden *is noted for the exceptionally tall lace headdress worn by its* women

Very safe for children. Loctudy's 12th-century church (hidden behind an unprepossessing 18th-century façade) is Breton Romanesque at its best. There are boat services from here to the Glénan isles and across the Anse de Bénodet.

The *pays* Bigouden has its own 'Land's End' (less visited than the better known Pointe du Raz, and therefore more enjoyable) at the **Pointe de Penmarc'h**, a dramatic place with a tall windswept lighthouse and a delicate 15th-century chapel sheltering below it beside a narrow creek. Both the Eckmühl lighthouse and the Notre Dame-de-la-Joie chapel are open to visitors. The black rocks of Penmarc'h, which means horse's head in Breton, are approached to best effect by the coastal road from the village of Guilvinec (which has a nice restaurant, the Centre) rather than the main D785 from Pont-l'Abbé which leads on to St. Guénolé. There are several good hotels here. On the road to the Anse de la Torche and its scenic headland and beach (scene of the world 'funboard' championships) there is the small but fascinating Finistère Museum of prehistory with an intriguing array of dolmens in the garden outside. The sense of times past is strong in this country of stone villages and megaliths constantly under the attack of the Atlantic winds and breakers.

The whole stretch of landscape between Quimper and the Bay of Audierne has this brooding, desolate atmosphere with its isolated hamlets, its lakes and half-ruined chapels, although in spring some of its fields are ablaze with the colours of tulips and daffodils. The calvary of Notre Dame-de-Tronoën, on a moorland hilltop 5km north of Penmarc'h, is said to be the oldest in Brittany and its lichened carvings of the Virgin Mary suckling the infant Jesus, the Last Supper and the Crucifixion are weathered enough to bear this out.

The River Goyen, which flows into the sea at **Audierne**, beneath a wooded hillside, marks the northern edge of the *pays* Bigouden. Tunny fishing boats still put out from the harbour here but it's a declining industry, a victim of more intensive deepsea fishing methods. The local fishermen are turning to the more lucrative trade of crayfish and lobsters, while Audierne is now in the mainstream of a growing industry, tourism, placed as it is at the confluence of the two main routes (D784 and D765) from Quimper and Douarnenez to the Pointe de Raz, the Land's End of Western Europe. Some small but splendidly appointed hotels, such as the Michelin-starred Le Goyen at the harbourside, testify to Audierne's continuing prosperity, while the nets and lobster pots spread out on the quays in front of handsome terraces of houses maintain the fishing port ambience. There is a fine beach 1km from the port and the local sightseeing includes a typically furnished Breton *chaumière* or cottage, ponds where fish and lobsters are stored live for the pot and an apiary with guided tours of the hives. It is worth making a small detour off the D784 as it continues westwards from Audierne to see the immaculate little chapel of St. Tugen.

A favourite mooring place for yachts is the Odet estuary

117

And so to the **Pointe du Raz**, where the main objective seems to be to trap tourists like lobsters. If you can tear yourself away from the welter of car parks and crêperies, souvenir stalls and postcard vendors, the views from the paths along the cliffs are nothing less than majestic. They are not for those without a head for heights, however, even though there are safety ropes to hang on to and guides. *Raz* means race and the cluster of lighthouses around the jagged shore here (not to mention the statue of Our Lady of Shipwrecks) are a warning of just how fierce and treacherous are the tidal rips between the Pointe and the Île de Sein which can be seen crouching on the horizon. Yachtsmen say that once they've passed south of the Raz du Sein the sun seems warmer and navigation easier, with the prospect of the delightful harbours, rivers and islands to come.

Pleasure boats make the crossing to the **Île de Sein** from Audierne in 70 minutes. The island now forms part of the Armorique Regional Nature Park. There isn't much to see there apart from the lighthouse (open to visitors) and an abundance of birdlife but Sein has earned its niche in history from the fact that in June 1940 when General de Gaulle broadcast his appeal from exile in London, every able-bodied man (and boy) from this island sailed for England after their *recteur* had urged them from the pulpit to answer the call. The whole population saw them off from the quay singing the *Marseillaise*.

Beyond the Pointe du Raz, going north, a narrow, lonely road skirts the Baie des Trépassés (Bay of the Dead), so called from the days when the bodies of Druid priests were ferried across it to their burial ground on the Île de Sein.

This stretch of coast to the Pointe du Van was sketched by Sarah Bernhardt, who attracted even in that wild spot an audience of louse-ridden urchins which, after various sorts of unpleasantness, she was obliged to disperse at the point of the jewelled revolver she always carried with her. Accompanied by her lady's maid and a steward, the world-famous actress must have been a rare sight. The scenery which attracted her, expanses of gorse and heather beside the jagged cliffs and the sometimes violent sea, is unchanged although a hotel stands there now—Miss Bernhardt stayed with Father Batifoule at Audierne, who was so well-fed that part of his dining table had to be cut away to accommodate his belly!

There are two routes to Douarnenez, the main one via Audierne and **Pont-Croix**, which rises in terraces above the River Goyen and has attracted its own school of artists. Picturesque streets and medieval houses cluster around the Romanesque-Gothic church of Notre Dame-de-Roscudon built between the 12th and 16th centuries and guided visits are organised in the summer months by the local Syndicat d'Initiative. Like most towns and villages of any consequence in Cornouaille, Pont-Croix has its *pardon* and fêtes: the Grand Pardon on 15 August and the Petit Pardon on the first Sunday in September. On the second Saturday in August there is a torchlit procession (Govel Noz) and during the same month a nautical festival and fishing competition. The nearby village of Confort (5.5km east on the D765) has a 16th-century church with twelve bells on a wheel which are rung as a novena to the Virgin Mary.

The alternative route between the

Pointe du Van and Douarnenez shadows the serrated northern shore of the peninsula, a kilometre or two inland. It is the southern rim of the Bay of Douarnenez, an expanse of water so beautiful that a 19th-century painting of it was auctioned for more than a million dollars by Sotheby's in New York early in 1989. The joy of this piece of coastline today is its inaccessibility, protected since the 1950s when Brittany's first major bird sanctuary was established at **Cap Sizun** squashing a plan to build an arterial road along the clifftops. Now it is the home of innumerable species of seabirds—cormorants, puffins, fulmars, razorbills and of course the ubiquitous herring gull—which can be observed in peace in their natural habitat of cliffs and sea. The reserve (tel 98.70.13.53) is open from March to the end of August from 10 to noon and 2 to 6pm. The best time to go is between 15 April and 15 July.

Douarnenez ranks only just below Concarneau as a deepsea fishing port and is a major tourist resort as well, noted for its fine beaches, especially the Plage des Dames, its sailing school, marina and year-round thalassotherapy centre in the neighbouring family resort of Tréboul on the western flank of the estuary across the Grand Pont. The mouth of the port is guarded by the green wooded island named after Tristan, Isolde's lover, to whom it was given by King Mark of Cornwall. Another legendary character associated with Douarnenez is King Gradlon—one explanation of its name is that it comes from the Breton *Douar Nevez* or 'new land' which replaced the king's lost city of Ys. Some say that this city lies beneath the waters of the bay and claim that its church bells can be heard ringing far out at sea. Others are equally convinced that Ys was engulfed by the Baie de Trépassés. Either way, a trip around the bay on board *Rosmeur* can be enhanced by listening to a recording of Debussy's piano prelude *La Cathédrale Engloutie* which was inspired by the legend. Less contemplative folk can try their hands at sea-fishing and visit the Criée, or fish auction, which is as impressive as those at Concarneau or Lorient. The Nouveau Port to the north of the Port du Rosmeur is the last word in technology with its fish factories and refrigerated warehouses. Away from the salty, fishy hubbub of the port there is a scenic footpath around the cliffs of Plomarc'h to the plage du Ris. Other places to visit are the church of Ploare, the chapels of St. Hélène and St. Michel, or, if one is weary of churches and chapels, the Laennec Gardens or the fascinating museum of old boats on the quai du Port Rhu.

Le Pénity Church at Locronan, named for St. Ronan who came from Ireland in the 5th century AD (see page 120)

Locronan, 10km inland east of Douar-nenez, takes its name from the Irish saint Ronan who preached and was buried here in the 5th century; its medieval buildings and the Celtic crosses in the churchyard are covered with moss and lichens, the crust of antiquity. Its beautiful cobbled square of Renaissance houses with an ancient well in the centre fronts the large church and chapel of Le Pénity with St. Ronan's hill behind. Down the hill is another, smaller church, Notre Dame-de-Bonne-Nouvelle, with a calvary and fountain. Locronan used to earn its living by weaving sailcloth for the *royale*, the Breton word for the French navy. If there is anything to criticise about the village today it is that it is almost *too* self-consciously pictureque and too full of 'artisans' boutiques selling Breton fishermen's sweaters and patisseries selling tins of *kouign-amann* and *crêpes dentelles*. The Fer à Cheval restaurant in the place Église serves a particularly tasty *cotriade*, a kind of fish stew containing oysters, clams, shrimps, sea snails and much else. The inn of the same name is 1km out ot town on the D63. Also very peaceful, the Manoir de Möellien, at Plonévez-Porzay 3km north-west on route C10, is a 17th-century stone building bearing the coat of arms of the family who built it, with the motto *Sell Pobl* (Breton for 'care about people'). This they do with good value meals and comfortable bedrooms in converted stone stables with French windows leading to the gardens, bright with hydrangeas in summer.

Brittany's dramatic 'Land's End' is the Pointe du Raz

Locronan has its *pardons*, including one which follows in the penitential steps of St. Ronan, but the best-known pardon in the whole of Brittany takes place at **Ste. Anne-la-Palud** at the edge of the Bay of Douarnenez, 8km to the north, at the end of August. The church is surrounded by green meadows where cows graze just a few hundred metres from the beach and the mass is said at a covered altar outside the building. This is no different from any of the *pardons* held throughout the length and breadth of Brittany during the summer except that pilgrims flock in their thousands to Ste. Anne-la-Palud. Overlooking the beach is one of Brittany's more luxurious hotels, named after the chapel.

Douarnenez to Brest

Heading north around the head of Douarnenez Bay, the next great peninsula jutting out into the Atlantic is that of Crozon, which on the map resembles the tongue of a dragon between the lower jaw of the Pointe du Raz and the snout which is Brest. Its gullet is the River Aulne flowing swiftly through **Châteaulin**, a highly regarded base for salmon fishermen. The little inn of the Ducs de Lin, 1.5km south on the old Quimper road, sleeps about a dozen and serves good meals cooked with fresh local produce. Châteaulin has shore facilities for visiting boats at the Port de Plaisance de Pen ar Pont (tel 98.73.25.34) where bicycles can be hired. Just 10km east, at **Pleyben**, is one of the most notable parish closes with its triumphal arch leading to a calvary on a huge vaulted base and an ossuary in the shadow of a vast 16th-century church.

The River Aulne passes just south of here on its sinuous course to Châteaulin from **Châteauneuf-du-Fao**, another *port de plaisance* and a relaxed little town built on a wooded ridge above the river, with one good, plain restaurant, the Relais de Cornouaille. There is a church memorial to 43 townsmen shot by the Nazis. East of here the river, now part of the Nantes-Brest Canal, is wide, deep and as serpentine as ever, coiling towards the forest of Laz and the lower slopes of the Montagnes Noires (which are hardly mountains, but rather hills) and back on itself until it eventually reaches the limit of navigation, the port of Carhaix. A few kilometres outside Châteauneuf-du-Fao on the road to Laz is the Belle Époque château of **Trévarez** standing in a wooded park with beautiful displays of camellias, rhododendrons and azaleas and open to visitors. Many festivals and cultural events are staged here, ranging from horse trials to *festivals de fleurs*.

Seaward of Châteaulin, a scenic route leads to **Ménez-Hom**—at 330m a mountain (but only just) yet among the highest points in the whole province. In 1944 it was used by the Germans as an outwork of their defences of Brest and was stormed by the American and Free French forces. A folklore festival is held on its summit on 15 August but at most other times the wide and windy moor is sparsely populated, in total contrast to the Pointe du Raz. And the views are just as magnificent in their own way, taking in all points of the compass, to the north the broad sheltered waters of the Rade de Brest, to the south the Bay of Douarnenez, to the east the valley of the Aulne cleaving the inland hills and to the west the Pointe de Penhir and the Cap de la Chèvre. What is more, it is

Ankou, the Coachman of Death

'In that country of scattered cromlechs and dolmens, every stone is a reminder of death and the worlds of the dead and the living are divided only by a thin veil,' writes Arthur Ransome in his chilling tale *Ankou* about two old men locked in a struggle for which the victor's prize is death. In Brittany the last man to die in the year in each parish becomes Ankou for that parish for the following year. The skeletal Ankou is the coachman of death who comes to convey his parishioners on their last journey. He carries a scythe, which he swings from left to right rather than from right to left, and he drives a heavy, groaning cart piled with bodies behind one emaciated horse or two animals, one well fed, the other mere skin and bones. There is no bribing the Ankou, who represents the implacable and arbitrary nature of death so familiar in a land of sailors and fishermen. Folklore tells how a certain blacksmith of Ploumillau spent time sharpening the Ankou's scythe instead of going to midnight mass, but he died next day just the same.

easy to reach the summit by car on the D83, a narrow road off the D887, or on foot 1.5km from the beautiful little Chapel of Ste. Marie at the bottom. St. Corentin is said to have spent his youth as a hermit in the woods at Plomodiern, the nearby village, living on wild berries, herbs and roots until God sent him the wonderful self-renewing fish. It was here that King Gradlon witnessed the miracle and his statue on horseback stands proudly in the 17th-century parish close at **Argol**, a hamlet in the centre of the Crozon peninsula.

West of Argol is the small town of **Crozon**, which although it provides the name for the whole peninsula has little to offer in the way of sightseeing. Its setting, however, is magnificent, fringed as it is to the south and west with a succession of coves and capes, points and promontories, every one with a sandy beach and a brilliant sea view. **Morgat** lies just to the south, nestling as it were in the crook of the protecting arm which reaches out towards the Cap de la Chèvre. Many visiting yachts seek the

shelter of its harbour beside the lighthouse and steep, wooded cliffs. Morgat is a lively, popular little resort with a selection of comfortable hotels and an outstandingly pretty beach. The 68m-high Pointe de Penhir, which is a bird sanctuary, provides a commanding view of the coast and its offshore islands.

The Crozon peninsula, a natural rampart for the great naval base of Brest, has attracted wave after wave of enemy invaders down the centuries and still displays the remnants of its fortifications from Vauban's 17th-century bastions to Hitler's Atlantic Wall. Even earlier, in 1590, Philip II of Spain sent an army to capture Brest in support of the Ligueurs, the Catholics opposing the Protestant Henry IV. The Crozon headland which they occupied for four years before they were defeated and sent packing is still called the Pointe des Espagnols. From

Overleaf: Douarnenez is said to have replaced the drowned city of Ys

123

Le Fret, at its base, a boat service operates to Brest on the opposite shore of the busy roadstead. The chapel of Notre Dame-de-Rocamadour at **Camaret** on the tip of the peninsula bears still a scar of a fierce engagement in 1694 when an Anglo-Dutch invasion force was repelled by a combination of French army and Breton 'home guard'. An English cannon ball sliced the top off the belfry and it has gone unrepaired in memory of that victory. The chapel is built on the *sillon*, the natural breakwater of pebbles which protects the harbour. It contains many model ships donated by sailors in thanksgiving for being saved from drowning. Camaret is very much a maritime town: the museum in the Vauban tower which

The ruins of Landevennec Abbey have been restored and house a museum of the monastic life

guards the harbour has among its exhibits the nameboard of the *Torrey Canyon* which broke up off the Scillies in 1967. It was in Camaret Bay in 1801 that an American nautical engineer named Robert Fulton demonstrated *Nautilus*, an oar-powered submarine which stayed underwater for six hours. Experiments by the French Navy later in that century no doubt influenced the Breton writer Jules Verne's novel, *Twenty Thousand Leagues under the Sea*.

The northern shore of the Crozon peninsula faces the immense sheltered waters of the Rade de Brest, where warships lie at anchor, overlooked by a naval air station. To visit the site of the abbey at **Landévennec** it is necessary to leave the main D791 route to follow a road along a hook-shaped promontory at the mouth of the Aulne to a pretty village among the trees. The ruins of the abbey founded in 485 by St. Guénolé and where King Gradlon is said to be buried are at the point of the hook and have been rebuilt and restored under the auspices of the Armorique Regional Nature Park as a museum where the history of Breton monasticism can be traced through the architecture and restored documents. After crossing the Aulne, the D791 forms a corniche beside the estuary of the River Faou where grey ranks of mothballed gunboats squat in the mud at low tide. The port of **Le Faou**, with its 16th-century covered market and green copper *poilu* as a war memorial, its main street lined with slate-fronted houses, is a place of character, undisturbed by the N165 autoroute thundering past on its way to Brest. The Vieille Renommée in the place Mairie is noted for its comfort and good traditional Breton cooking but if it is full up (as it often is in summer) try the Relais de la Place next door which is also excellent value.

The Brest road carves its way northwards through unimaginably lovely countryside to **Daoulas** where it is worth pausing to visit perhaps the most interesting abbey church in the whole province. Indeed, its Romanesque cloister is the only complete surviving example in Brittany. Its carved figures, whether of lichened, time-worn grey stone or brilliantly coloured wood, are a joy to behold, as is the calvary, the fretted tower with its trio of bells, the fountain and the oratory. Visitors can wander around the ruins and the park with its medicinal herb garden. The abbey was founded by St. Colomban monks in AD500 and was powerful until the 10th century when it fell into ruin for the first time. Augustinian priors rebuilt it in the 12th century and it remained influential until the Revolution. Now, in the ownership of the Département of Finistère, it is enjoying another renaissance. In the summer of 1988 it was the scene of a major international exhibition of artefacts from the Bronze Age to which 52 European museums contributed.

After Daoulas, the N165 swings westward across the strawberry fields before crossing the estuary of the Elorn to the outskirts of Brest. **Plougastel-Daoulas**, at the heart of this area, is famous not only for the liqueur that it produces from the strawberries but also for a fine calvary which was carved in the early 17th century in thanksgiving for deliverance from a plague.

Brest to Roscoff

Brest is to the French Navy—the *royale* in Brittany— what Portsmouth or Plymouth are to the British. It stands at the edge of one of the best naturally protected roadsteads in the world, the Rade de Brest. Entered through the narrows called the Goulet de Brest and guarded by the Presqu'île de Crozon, these waters have sheltered generations of warships from the wooden walls launched by the Duchess Anne against the fleet of Henry VIII and Napoleon's ships-of-the-line blockaded by Nelson's navy to the pride of Hitler's fleet in World War II. The battleship *Bismarck* was heading for Brest when it was sunk. As the key to the Channel approaches Brest was always important in naval strategy. Even today the naval dockyard on both banks of the River Penfeld is kept under strict security. (Guided tours are restricted to French nationals and cameras are prohibited.) A constant stream of tankers and other commercial shipping comes and goes and although Brest is hardly a mecca for tourists it has berths for a hundred visiting yachts at the Port du Plaisance du Moulin Blanc. The waters of the *rade* give access to the rivers Aulne and Elorn, both with excellent cruising facilities and Brest is a centre for nautical sports and events.

It is a new city of concrete and glass which rose from the ashes and debris of the old after the six-week siege of 1944. The American General Patton, a tank man, gave the simple order 'Take Brest!' but the German garrison commander Hermann Ramcke told his men

A holy fountain stands within the cloister of Daoulas Abbey

to fight to the death and the city was finally captured on 18 September 1944 after house-to-house fighting. Hardly anything survived of ancient Brest other than the château, now the headquarters of the Préfecture Maritime, and the 15th-century Tanguy tower on the opposite bank of the Penfeld. Both are dwarfed by the largest vertical lift bridge in Europe, the Pont de Recouvrance, which spans the river just to the north of them. It is possible to walk on this bridge, for a stupendous view of the arsenal and the roadstead. Brest has nothing to compare with Portsmouth's trio of historic ships, *Mary Rose*, *Victory* and *Warrior*, but the museum in the Tour Tanguy does provide a graphic impression of the old town, especially of its prison or *bagne* which was the forerunner of Devil's Island off the coast of

South America. The great harbour was built by convict chain gangs between the mid-18th and 19th centuries. If anyone escaped, the surrounding countryside was warned by cannon blast from the ramparts, a sound that came to be known as *tonnerre de Brest*—Brest thunder. Brest-Guipavas Airport, northeast of the city, has direct links with London, Paris and the south of France.

Although at first sight this industrial and commercial city seems completely out of place surrounded by wild, lonely seashore and grey little towns and villages at the western extremity of France, 596km from Paris, in fact it is very much part of Breton culture. Its Université de Bretagne Occidentale promotes the study of Celtic languages and history and among its cultural events is a summer festival of stories and legends.

One of the main attractions of Brest is a cruise around the *rade* by Vedettes Armoricaines and there are trips through the Goulet around Pointe de St. Mathieu to **le Conquet**, an ancient fishing village with a deep harbour 24km west of the city, and beyond to the offshore islands of Molène and **Ouessant** (Ushant), part of the Parc Régional d'Armorique. There is also a car ferry. It's a two-hour voyage to Ushant, for centuries the landfall for homecoming French ships from the Indies or the Americas, an island that is worth visiting for its scenery and its impressive array of lighthouses: La Jument, Kéréon, Le Créac'h and La Stiff. Any or all of these offer the visitor a 'Coup d'oeil fantastique,' as the French guide puts it. In a north-easterly wind, the bay of Lampaul provides a safe anchorage for yachts.

North from Le Conquet and its broad Atlantic panoramas, the Côte du Léon is pierced with a succession of long shallow estuaries which take their names from the Welsh 'Aber'. A corniche is out of the question. Instead, the main roads radiate like the spokes of wheel from Brest and the rim consists of unconnected sections of coastal road. Although some of these stretches, such as those around Lampaul-Ploudalmézeau and Lampaul-Plouarzel, where the Auberge du Kruguel serves delectable salmon, are attractive, they are quite different from the wooded cliffs of Cornouaille. The bare heath, scattered with dolmens and menhirs, rolls gently down to the sea. The roads from Penfoul to Kersaint and along the shores of Aber Benoît and Aber Wrac'h have a wild beauty of their own. It was off **Portsall**, with its tiny, almost landlocked harbour, that the *Amoco Cadiz* ran aground in 1978, polluting the whole

coast. Yet today these villages with outlandish names look as if nothing has changed in centuries; there are few if any concessions to the demands of tourism. For some, this is the attraction: lonely beaches, quiet estuaries and creeks, few hotels other than small unpretentious, family-run establishments, no casinos. The Hôtel Baie des Anges at **Aber Wrac'h** is a good example of the sort of comfortable little place to which 'regulars' return year after year. This is a minute village at the mouth of the sea loch, with fields running down to the water, where once poor farmers hung lamps on the horns of their cattle to lure ships on to the rocks. The Île Vierge lighthouse, the tallest in Europe (77m, 392 steps to the top) soars above the estuary and sailors waiting for the right tide and winds to make passage through the Chenal du Four between Ushant and the mainland gather over cognac in the Café du Port. It is difficult to believe that such a relaxed place can be found less than 30km from the traffic roar of Brest.

By the standards of this far corner of Finistère, **Brignonan-Plages** is a lively resort, appealing to families who want a good sandy beach where the water is shallow and safe for children's bathing. It is divided into coves by outcrops of rock and there are sheltering dunes so that everyone can find a secluded spot to call their own. The road to Brignogan from Quimper passes through **Landerneau**, where medieval houses line the bridge over the Elorn, and **Le Folgoët**, on the outskirts of Lesneven, which gives its name to a curious legend. It means literally 'Fool of the Wood' and the fool in question is said to have lived under a tree, begging for his food and continually invoking the name of the

The Armorique Regional Nature Park

This is one of 25 regional nature parks in France. It extends over 95,000 hectares of the offshore islands of Sein and Ouessant (Ushant) as well as a large part of the Crozon peninsula, the Aulne estuary and the inland uplands of the Monts d'Arrée, where, somewhat paradoxically, it includes the nuclear reactor at Brennills. Not, in many people's eyes, a boon to the environment. However, the aim of the park's administration made up of the elected representatives of 32 rural communes, the *département* of Finistère, the regional government and the city of Brest is stated as being to promote and develop tourism while preserving an environment which includes some of the most beautiful coastal scenery in Europe, rocks which date back to the genesis of the planet itself and a rich heritage of megaliths and religious architecture.

A journey through the park provides an opportunity to see deer and wild boar roaming free in the woods at **Ménez-Meur**, **Hanvec**, and beaver colonies at **Brennilis** and **Loqueffret** along the rivers Ellez, Roudouhir and Roudoudour. There are study centres and museums in restored abbeys and ancient watermills. A former railway station at **Scrignac** houses a hunting museum and provides training for hunters as well as behavioural studies of various kinds of game. On the banks of the Aulne at **Trégarven** the history of schooling in rural Brittany from the 1880s is presented in a school built at the turn of the century in a playground planted with lime trees. The wild, rock-strewn moorland hills reach their summit at the **Montagne St. Michel** where a chapel stands at an altitude of 380m commanding a wide panorama that includes the great reservoir with the nuclear station beside it. At the foot of the mountain at **Brasparts** many well-known craftworkers exhibit their output in a craft museum. There are hostels for groups visiting the regional park and itineraries for hiking, horse-riding and trekking in gipsy-style caravans (tel 98.68.81.71).

Virgin Mary. After he died and was buried around the year 1358 a single white lily sprouted from his grave with the words 'Ave Marie' in gold on its petals. Shortly afterwards, Duke Jean IV, celebrating his succession after his victory at the Battle of Auray, built a chapel on the site which is the scene of a colourful *pardon* at the beginning of September. Duchess Anne visited Le Folgoët on a pilgrimage of thanksgiving for the recovery of her second husband Louis XII, King of France, from a serious illness. Every year she sent gifts of jewels, cloth-of-gold vestments and alms and provided the money to complete the great 15th-century basilica which stands in a large open space. The interior is pleasing, with a fountain behind the main altar and a rood screen carved from granite. Stained glass windows at the eastern end tell the story of the 'The Fool', otherwise known as Salomon the Mad, and an urn given by the Black Watch and containing soil from Brittany, Picardy and Scotland commemorates Celtic brothers-in-arms of World War I.

Le Folgoët is only 35km away from the port of **Roscoff** at which thousands of visitors arrive from Plymouth and Cork by Brittany Ferries. The majority seem to drive their cars straight out of town, overlooking the fact that Roscoff is also a graceful resort and spa with many good hotels and the Maison Rouge tropical gardens where cacti, palm trees and myriad flowers from the South Pacific and South America flourish. Its climate is softened by the Gulf Stream, proof of which can be seen in a huge fig tree planted early in the 17th century in the garden of the newly founded Capucin Convent and still producing masses of fruit. Granite columns support this tree that was well over a century old when Bonnie Prince Charlie landed here after fleeing from Skye. An earlier visitor, Mary Queen of Scots, spent a night in Roscoff at the age of five in the summer of 1548 on her way to Paris to become engaged to the future King of France as the basis for an alliance of the two kingdoms against England. The voyage from the Clyde in violent storms took 18 days and it is on record that the little girl was less seasick than most of the other passengers.

The tropical gardens illustrate the link between Brittany's farming and seafaring traditions, the sailing ships return from faraway places with specimens of exotic plants. Roscoff has also long been a centre for the study of marine biology. The Aquarium Charles Pérez at the Institute of Oceanology is open to visitors as well as students. It is a grey town, entirely built of granite. Even the canons set in the 16th-century church tower—to warn off the English, it's said—are of stone. They point in two directions: towards the northern horizon over which today's car ferries appear and westwards up the channel between the mainland and the **Île de Batz**. It is a short boat trip from the har-

bour to this little island where St. Paul-Aurelian subdued a dragon by tying his stole around its neck as a kind of leash before leading it to the shore and making it jump into the sea. The stole, and a reliquary containing some of his bones, are preserved in the relatively modern (19th century) church on Batz. He ended his days at the monastery here and the little fields, walled with that same grey stone and manured with seaweed, remain blissfully undisturbed.

The town named after this saint, **St. Pol-de-Léon**, stands a little way back from the sea just south of Roscoff. It has two magnificient Gothic churches. One is the twin-towered former cathedral, dating back to the 13th century, and the other the Kreisker chapel, whose 77m-high spire commands the coast and the seemingly endless fields of artichokes, onions and cauliflowers behind. The deepwater harbour at Roscoff was built for the more efficient export of the produce from the Ceinture Dorée, making the bereted vendors who used to swarm across the Channel with their bicycles strung about with onions a threatened species. St. Pol is the market town and the bishops traditionally took a keen interest in the commerce on their doorstep—the last of the line, Monseigneur de la Marche, was known as the Potato Bishop for his fight against taxes on crops. The first Bishop of Léon was of course St. Pol (or Paul-Aurelian), who was born in England, educated in Wales with St. Samson and crossed the Channel to Brittany early in the 6th century. The cathedral contains his head, a finger and a bone from his arm. It is said he lived to be 104. There is a lovely rose window in the south transept of the cathedral and some intricately carved 16th-century choir stalls.

Morlaix lies a few kilometres inland on the estuary of the River Dossen and its most outstanding feature is the huge arched railway viaduct spanning the valley. The locked basin in the heart of the town is packed with pleasure craft and visiting yachts in summer and gabled, half-timbered houses and cobbled streets climb steep hills from the quays. The house where the Duchess Anne stayed on her pilgrimage of thanksgiving around the Duchy in 1505 and the church of St. Mélanie are among the sights to be seen. Like St. Malo, Morlaix was once the base of corsairs, who in 1522 sacked Bristol. In reprisal, an English fleet landed at Morlaix. Most of its citizens were away attending a festival at Guingamp and the invaders, meeting little opposition, helped themselves to everything they wanted and got very drunk. They were still sleeping it off when the townspeople returned and put many of them to the sword: hence the Morlaix motto 'If they bite you, bite them'. The Château de Taureau on the Pointe de Penal-Lann where the estuary flows into Morlaix bay was built by the citizens in 1542 to repel English invaders, who nowadays take the tide up to the town centre without any opposition whatever. A 15km drive along the corniche to **Carantec**, a happy little resort with a spotlessly clean beach and a casino, is equally enjoyable.

For those who don't wish to explore the Côte du Léon, the inland route from Cornouaille to Morlaix passes through some of the best scenery of the Argoat, across the moors of the regional park to

Previous page: The Parc Régional d'Armorique contains wonderful vantage points, as at the Roc Trévezel

a hilly landscape full of rushing trout streams and waterfalls with woods of oak, beech and pine, more like the Alps than Brittany. These are the Monts d'Arrée, of which the highest point (the highest in Brittany, in fact) is St. Michel at 384m. This relatively modest mountain commands a memorable panorama of the Far West, especially from the escarpment of Roc Trévezel. This is fascinating country to explore on foot or by bicycle, by car or by horse-drawn caravan, especially in springtime when the whole of Finistère becomes a garden of camellia and mimosa, the rhododendrons and azaleas burst into bloom and paths and lanes are fringed with blossom of gorse and broom. In summer hortensias grow everywhere, adding vivid splashes of colour to whitewashed and grey stone cottages. Some of the places to see around the charming little town of **Huelgoat** are the Chaos du Moulin for its fanastic granite outcrops and the Grotte du Diable where the river dives underground. It is reached on foot down a steep, winding path—this is walking country. A curiosity of the area is the 100-tonne rock which sways when it is touched but is never toppled by the sometimes fierce Breton winds.

Just off the road descending from the Monts d'Arrée to Morlaix is **Pleyber-Christ** noted for the great triumphal arch dedicated to the fallen of World War I and leading to a fine Gothic Renaissance church which seems to symbolise the devout Christianity of the Breton people and can serve as a starting point for a circuit of that other symbol of piety, the unique parish closes, most of which lie within easy driving distance from here (see Box). The best starting point, however, is probably from Landivisiau to the west, which

Parish Closes

The ornate Breton parish close is the ultimate display of that religious fervour which is expressed throughout the countryside in wayside shrines and granite crucifixes and calvaries at crossroads. They were built to demonstrate not only the piety but also the prosperity of farming communities who had done well out of growing hemp for the canvas that was used to make sails, an important home and export market. The parish close almost always takes the form of a church and a walled square entered through a triumphal arch and including an ossuary or charnel house where the bones of the dead are stored and a *calvaire* representing scenes from the Crucifixion with intricate stone carving.

There was an element of competition between villages and the finest examples of parish closes are concentrated in the valley of the River Elorn from just south of Morlaix towards Brest, which was a particularly prosperous agricultural area. The best starting point is at the small market town of **Landivisiau**, where the church has a 16th-century porch large enough to hold parish meetings in and a holy well dedicated to its patron, St. Thivisiau. Its water is piped to communal washing tubs, still used here and there in Brittany even in the age of automatic washing machines. **Lampaul-Guimiliau** the village just 4km to the south-east once had a chuch spire to rival St. Pol-de-Léon's in height at 70m but it was truncated by lightning during a storm at the beginning of the 19th century and was never rebuilt. The 16th-century building in a typical *enclos* contains some fascinating painted statues (including one of St. Pol leading the dragon by his stole wound around its neck) but its calvary pales into insignificance alongside that of the neighbouring village of **Guimiliau**. Completed in 1588, its granite figures of the Disciples, the Holy Family, the legendary Katell-Gollet, damned for all eternity for her immorality, and a lady in court dress believed to represent Mary Queen of Scots, radiate life and energy.

The parish close at **St. Thégonnec**, a little way to the north-east, is of a later, 17th-century period when the Breton Renaissance had reached full flower and its calvary teems with action and character. King Henri IV who remarked 'Paris is worth a Mass' when he cynically converted to Catholicism is portrayed, grinning grotesquely, as one of the tormentors of Christ on the cross. The ossuary at St. Thégonnec, built between 1676 and 1682, is incomparable with its columns and pediment. Between Landivisiau and Landernau, the lonely village of **La Martyre**, which in the Middle Ages was the venue of a great annual fair where Mediterranean wine and fruit was bartered for timber, fish and hemp from northern Europe, is the birthplace of the *enclos paroissiaux* in the 15th century. The calvary here is part of the triumphal arch and the south porch added to the 11th-century church in 1460 is a Breton history lesson in itself, richly carved with saints and peasants, shields and coats-of-arms, surmounted by the Nativity.

There are parish closes also at Bodilis, La Roche-Maurice, Ploudiry, Locmélar, Plouneour-Ménez and Commana and one of the finest of all at **Sizun**, where the arch is truly triumphant with three monumental spans with a long gallery above and the interior of the grey granite church is flamboyantly painted and gilded.

nearby has the greatly admired château of Kerjean, set in a lovely park, its Renaissance courtyard within the massive walls surrounded by elegant buildings. The rooms contain some of the best examples to be found of period Breton furniture and performances of Breton music, song and dance are given regularly in the Grand Gallery.

Its ornate calvary makes Guimiliau one of the most interesting Breton 'parish closes'

Morlaix is dominated by this great granite viaduct

8
From Morlaix to St. Brieuc

Morlaix to Tréguier

Morlaix, like most of the larger towns in Brittany, is fighting against an ever-rising tide of road traffic and its somewhat complicated one-way system can be confusing. It is all too easy to find oneself, as I did, on the expressway to St. Brieuc rather than the road to the Pink Granite Coast and be obliged to travel several kilometres before finding an exit. However, the Côte de Granit Rose is certainly worth taking time and trouble to see. Immediately east of the Bay of Morlaix from the scenic panoramas of the Pointe de Primel the coast is less indented than that to the west. The tide goes out a long way leaving thousands of hectares of firm flat sand for jogging, riding, volleyball, or *boules*. Just inland, next to **Plougasnou**, is a little village with the curious name of **St. Jean-du-Doigt**, which comes from the custody in its parish close of the right forefinger of John the Baptist. Sceptics may raise an eyebrow at this, but the locals remain convinced that the article kept in a box by the priest is what it purports to be. It was brought, they say, from Jerusalem to Normandy where it was miraculously transferred to

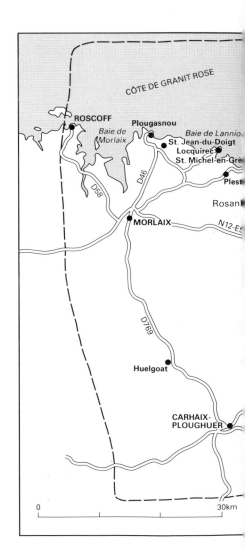

138

the person of a young man from Plou-gasnou who carried it home unwittingly to the accompaniment of church bells ringing of their own accord and trees bowing down. A new church was built to accommodate the relic and Duke Jean V himself laid the first stone on 1 August 1440. The finger is believed to have curative powers which has made St. Jean-du-Doigt a pilgrimage centre

and the scene of an annual *pardon* for the past 550 years.

Just down the coast is the attractive little port of **Locquirec**, which although it can be choked with people and traffic at weekends, is usually quiet. It has a church dedicated by the Knights of Malta and a walled harbour overlooked by a family-run hotel, the Port. The prices are reasonable, even more so at

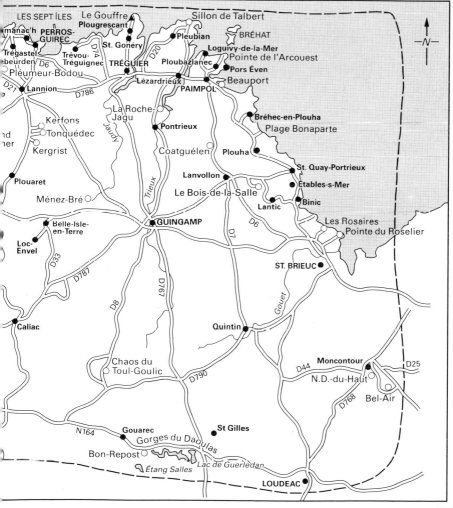

Les Algues nearby, which serves crêpes, pizzas and enormous dishes of *moules marinière* with inexpensive Muscadet to wash them down. Up the hill, the Pennenez Hôtel has comfortable rooms, some with balconies looking down on to the stone-tiled roofs of the houses clustered around the harbour, but no restaurant. Locquirec faces the Baie de Lannion and is flanked by numerous golden beaches and dunes with gorse-covered headlands. The Corniche de l'Armorique winds around the bay and there are some pleasant camping sites at the edge of the sea such as the Bellevue with facilities near at hand for fishing, tennis, minigolf and Motocross. Roadside stalls are piled high with produce straight from the market gardens and there are masses of hortensias (hydrangeas) and other flowers everywhere, in neat little gardens and growing wild on the road verges. The little seaside hamlet of St. Efflam takes its name from an Irish hermit who landed here in AD470, killed a monster and is remembered by a pretty chapel with a domed fountain.

This is holiday Brittany at its most welcoming. Between **Plestin**, whose 16th-century church was blown up by the Germans in 1944 and has since been rebuilt, and the beach resort of **St. Michel-en-Grève**, the road is overhung on one side by a mass of rock 80m high called the Grand Rocher. For those who are feeling energetic there is a path to the top, rewarded by a fine view of the Lieue de Grève, the 4km sweep of the beach on the other side of the coast road. This is the grandest of beaches,

Locquirec is a pretty port with super beaches all around

which widens to 2km when the tide goes out leaving boats high and dry and sands firm enough to drive or ride on. Moreover, it is watered by streams running down through wooded valleys from the hills dotted with a dozen or more out-of-the-way hamlets. Trout fishing is a major pastime.

It is only 11km from St. Michel-en-Grève to **Lannion**, a hillside town with an airport and the Pléumeur-Bodou satellite communications centre to the north which is open to visitors from April to October and includes a planetarium show. Lannion is better known, however, for its many ancient, half-timbered houses around the place du Centre and the narrow alleyways leading off it, and for the 12th-century Brélévenez church built by the Knights Templars, perched high above the port on the banks of the River Léguer and approached by 142 granite steps. From Lannion route D786 runs straight across country to Tréguier but to see the pink rocks that give this northern coast of Brittany its name, head north-west on the D21, then the D65. The Côte de Granit Rose really begins at **Trébeurden**, whose hilly streets look down on beaches that are divided by great clumps and outcrops of rosy rock which seems to glow in the sun and continues around the heavily indented corniche Bretonne to Perros-Guirec by way of Trégastel. The same distinctive tint can be seen in the boulders strewn over the landscape and the dozens of rocky islands peppering the coastal waters and in dolmens and menhirs such as the unusual Christian monument to St. Duzec. That newer phenomenon, the telecommunications 'golf-ball', sits on the open heath outside the village of **Pléumeur-Bodou**, as if some giant had

The rocks of the Pink Granite coast have been weathered into many shapes, some as recognisable as 'Father Trébeurden'

misjudged his tee-shot from the course which lies just to the north of it. The 18-hole, par 72 St. Sansom golf course (tel 96.23.87.34) reflects the growing popularity of this sport throughout France. You will need a good map to find it as it is hidden in a maze of hedge-walled lanes but it occupies a delightful site on high, undulating ground with wide views. It has excellent greens and some challenging holes, especially the 15th, 16th and 17th. The clubhouse is new and other sporting facilities to hand include snooker, a swimming pool and two tennis courts. Offshore the multi-coloured sails of funboards and yachts making the most of the prevailing westerly winds draw ever-changing patterns on the delphinium sea. Sport and leisure is always part of the scene on this coast and there are several attractive

camping sites in lush, flower-filled surroundings.

Just 3km from St. Sansom golf course, **Trégastel-Plage** is the best of bases for exploring the Pink Granite Coast and the roseate rocks here have been worn into an endless variety of fantastic shapes over centuries of assault by the sea, wind and rain. They form lagoons and pools around the coves and beaches. There is a seawater aquarium containing tropical as well as Breton species inside a pink granite cave. This quiet resort, enlivened somewhat in summer by festivals of jazz and rock, has a range of good hotels, none of which is outrageously expensive. On the other side of two rocky headlands which stretch out like a lobster's claws is the resort of **Ploumanac'h**, similar in style to Trégastel and a perfect place for children to play whatever is the latest version of 'Cowboys and Indians'. The beach is small and sometimes crowded but it is easy to escape among the pink boulders. A path climbs from the beach along the coast to the lighthouse.

The 6km cliff-walk from Ploumanac'h to **Perros-Guirec** is romantically

A telecommunications radome sits like a giant golf ball on the heath at Pléumeur-Bodou

named the Customs officers' path (Sentier des Douaniers). Perros-Guirec is a big, bustling port and resort with not one but two wide arcs of golden sand (the beaches of Trestraou and Trestrignel) fringing a rock-studded bay, its harbour packed with yachts. It has 2,000 self-catering units, 800 beds in a variety of hotels to suit all pockets, 60 restaurants and crêperies, two conference centres, a casino and a seawater therapy centre. Its four camping sites include the Municipal Ernest Renan on the outskirts at the edge of the sea and with an expanse of landlocked water for safe windsurfing. The tourist office at 21 place de l'Hôtel de Ville (tel 96.23.21.15) reflects the town's determination to pack the visitors in. Remote or peaceful it is not, yet it is still recognisably Breton. A large scale *pardon* is held on 15 August and the 15th-century chapel of Notre Dame-de-la-Clarté attracts many sightseers. Its bell not only summoned the parishioners to prayer but warned them of English pirates approaching.

Boats operate from Perros-Guirec to Guernsey and Jersey and there are trips around a much nearer set of islands, the **Sept Îles**, a bird sanctuary where the colony of gannets numbers 6,000 couples and where guillemots, cormorants, puffins and even small penguins have their nest. Landing is permitted only on Monk Isle. Les Vedettes Blanches (tel 96.23.22.47) go there daily from Trestraou beach.

The ever increasing growth of tourism seems to have bypassed the stretch of coast east of Perros-Guirec between the

Thalassotherapy—the Sea Cure

Brittany's 20th-century answer to many of the complaints that were traditionally taken care of by the Seven Healing Saints—rheumatic and arthritic aches and pains and nervous tensions—makes full use of the region's sea water, bracing air and invigorating climate. It is called thalassotherapy, a slightly daunting modern word for what is basically a good, old-fashioned 'sea cure' refined, developed and scientifically controlled. Bretons have been aware for centuries of the medicinal powers of seawater and seaweed but it is only fairly recently that tourists have been let into the secret. Thalassotherapy centres are attached to comfortable holiday hotels around both the north and south coasts. (Details of thalassotherapy centres in Brittany can be found in the Practical Information section at the back of this book.)

The régime is less severe than that usually imposed at the hydro or health farm and allows plenty of time for sightseeing, shopping, eating out, sunbathing or whatever. Your stay begins with a consultation with a doctor to establish what your particular problems are and to work out the most suitable treatment and timetable. This may include individual or communal exercises in jet pools, massages, seawater baths, treatment with high-pressure hoses and a variety of extras such as slimming cures, beauty treatments and yoga exercises. The latest form of thalassotherapy concentrates on the teeth and gums, using salt water to good effect.

The fantastic pink rocks at Île Renote, Trégastel, look towards Les Sept Îles

two Pointes du Château. The only resort of note is **Port-Blanc**, whose stone-built villas front a sandy beach, with rocks all around and innumerable small islands offshore. **Trévou-Tréguignec** also has a couple of nice, quiet hotels. Although but a short drive from upbeat Perros-Guirec it seems like a remote area, good for long walks and contemplation of nature. This would have been the terrain which greeted the first migrants from Britain in the 5th and 6th centuries, stony and unforgiving. The coastal path GR34 offers a succession of inspiring views, culminating in the most spectacular of all at the easternmost Pointe du Château near **Plougrescant**.

At **Le Gouffre** is one of the most intriguing little houses in Brittany, sandwiched

between two great slabs of rock surrounded by an almost circular stone wall on a narrow neck of land with water on both sides. As an example of architecture and landscape merged into one it is superb. The trail then turns southwards, following the wide course of the River Jaudy to the inland city of Tréguier. At **St. Gonéry** there is an unexpected treat in a little chapel with an oddly twisted spire and an outdoor pulpit. Inside, the wooden roof of the nave is painted with vivid scenes from the Bible.

Tréguier's fascinating Cathedral invites a visit (see page 146)

At Le Gouffre landscape and architecture merge into one

Tréguier to St. Brieuc

The old town of **Tréguier** with half-timbered houses, a market square and stone-spired cathedral invites the traveller to pause for some sightseeing and perhaps a meal, even to stay overnight. The Hôtel L'Estuaire occupies a rambling old building at the quayside. The rooms are basic but the dining room on the first floor has big windows through which to watch the boats coming and going on the tide while enjoying a good meal at a very reasonable price. Cruises and fishing trips are available. The streets climb steeply from the port to the town centre, dominated by the cathedral spire, as full of holes as a pepperpot to diminish the effect of a sometimes ferocious wind, which it has withstood for centuries.

Although its patron is St. Tugdual, who founded the bishopric in the 6th century, Tréguier Cathedral glorifies the memory of the only post-medieval Breton saint, Yves. Being a friend of the poor and, more remarkably, a lawyer, he is the best loved of them all. Every year on 19 May, the anniversary of his death and also his canonisation, lawyers from all over the world come to

Tréguier to honour him in a procession to the manor house of Ker-Martin where he was born in 1253. At the head of the procession a jewelled casket containing the skull of the saint is carried. When Yves returned to his native city as the *Officiel* appointed by the Bishop, after many years of study in Paris and Orléans, he was distinguished by the fairness of his judgements, often taking the side of the poor against the rich and powerful *seigneurs*. A wood carving in the south transept shows him standing between the rich and the poor. He also fed and clothed paupers and orphans, while wearing a hair shirt himself and eating the most meagre of diets. He preached in churches far and wide and prayed constantly. When he died at 49, enormous crowds gatherd at the cathedral to prostrate themselves before his coffin, weeping and wailing.

Yves was buried in the cathedral in 1303 and was canonised 44 years later. Duke Jean V built a chapel in the cathedral so that he could be buried next to St. Yves. Both tombs were destroyed during the Revolution and the present ones are 19th century replacements. There are three statues of the saint, 16th and 17th century. The Duke's Chapel leads off the Gothic nave and choir constructed in the 14th century with repeated interruptions from the Hundred Years' War and the Breton Wars of Succession. But there are remains of the earlier Romanesque cathedral, and the columns of Hastings Tower, built in the 11th and 12th centuries, are decorated with Celtic motifs. The original stained glass windows were all destroyed during the Revolution. The replacements are the work of M. de Sainte-Marie, representing scenes from the Old and New Testaments and the lives of the saints. The Bell Tower, the Duke's Chapel and the delectable Cloister are in the Decorated style.

Tréguier Cathedral is packed with interest even for those who are not dedicated sightseers and a one-page typed factsheet in English is freely available as a guide. St. Yves isn't the only notable son of Tréguier. The 19th-century philosopher and religious historian Ernest Renan, who was born here in 1823, shocked and outraged the church by daring to suggest in his *Life of Jesus* that Christ was just a man, however incomparable. Renan's birthplace just off the square is a museum of his life, work and journeys and contains his school desk and a report critical of his 'absent-mindedness' in church.

Between the Jaudy estuary and that of the Trieux lies the little visited promontory that ends in the Sillon de Talbert, pointing out to sea like a long finger. There are no major roads in this isolated corner of northern Brittany, just winding lanes and small hamlets with strange sounding names. There is a quiet and pleasant camping site by the sea at **Pleubian** but no restaurants or hotels to rate a mention in the guide books. Yachts sailing along the impressive northern coast often sail up the wide River Trieux past two lighthouses standing like sentinels on the shore to **Lézardrieux** to anchor for the night or tie up at the quay. The view upriver from the bridge at Lézardrieux towards the forest of Lan Cert is worth stopping for and 9km away, on a bluff high above the river, is the 15th-century **Château La Roche-Jagu**. It lies just off the D787 route from Lézardrieux to Pontrieux and has been carefully restored with particular attention to the carving and joinery

of its internal timbers. It is open all year and often stages exhibitions and *animations* for children.

At the head of the Trieux estuary in a secluded creek is a tiny and quite unspoilt fishing village called **Loguivy-de-la-Mer**. It has no beach, there are plenty of those elsewhere, but an isolated megalith is within easy walking distance. The coastal path GR34 winds around the estuary and across to the **Pointe de l'Arcouest** with lovely views of the coast, the sea and the scattering of islands. The largest of these on the horizon is the island of Bréhat, which can be reached in ten minutes by boat from the little lobster fishing port at the Pointe, which used to be considered the ultimate escape until it was 'discovered' and there is now a hotel Le Barbu with a swimming pool in the garden. The **Île de Bréhat** remains free from motor traffic, which is banned, although it has some basic roads and two modest hotels. The island is blessed with a delightfully mild climate and even in winter mimosa and myrtle bloom in gardens and fields protected by stone walls. Fig trees grow happily outdoors. The beaches are mostly shingly. The islanders will tell you that it was one of their forebears, a Captain Coatanlen, who described the New World to Columbus eight years *before* the celebrated explorer went there himself. The local fishermen were already well acquainted with the Newfoundland Banks. The dominance of maritime activity in the lives of Breton families is emphasised by a cemetery wall in the hamlet of **Ploubazlanec** astride the pretty coastal road from Pointe de l'Arcouest to Paimpol. It bears the names of all the local men lost at sea over the

centuries. Another sad reminder is the Widows Cross at **Pors Éven** where the local women would gather to await the return of their men from voyages. **Paimpol** at the western extremity of the Gulf of St. Malo was the setting for Pierre Loti's *Le Pêcheur d'Islande*, as great a classic of the sea as Herman Melville's *Moby Dick*. Loti's real name was Louis Marie Julien Viaud and he knew the lives of the 'Islandais' well, having served at sea himself from 1867 to 1910, a captain for his last four years. He died in 1923. Although the Newfoundland and Icelandic cod fishing is now history, Paimpol continues to celebrate it every year in mid-July with the Fêtes des Terre-Nuevas et des Islandais. The port at the heart of the town remains packed with fishing boats and yachts and Guilben Cape, jutting out in to the bay, is the home of the National School of Merchant Marine. The Museum of the Sea relates local maritime history and that of the fishing off Iceland and there is a floating museum in an old schooner *Mad Atao* now classified as an historical monument. Another such monument is the house built by the corsair Pierre Corouge Kersaux in 1793 by Paimpol harbour wall. Kersaux became an enthusiastic revolutionary and president of the Tribunal de Commerce Maritime de Paimpol which has wide powers regarding armament as well as commerce. The handsome grey stone mansion, whose dining room and bedrooms overlook the harbour, is now

There are regular boats to the island of Bréhat from the Pointe de l'Arcouest

The cloister of Tréguier is a good example of the Decorated style

a comfortable hotel, Le Repaire de Kerroc'h. Despite its wealth of history, Paimpol is decidedly not living in the past. Indeed it bubbles with vitality, especially when the whole town centre becomes one great open-air market selling every kind of modern man-made product as well as the produce of the ocean and the surrounding countryside. It is a cultural experience in itself.

The ruins of **Beauport Abbey**, founded in the 13th century by the monks of La Lucerne, stand amidst trees 2km south of Paimpol on route D786 beside the bay at Kérity. Four rooms of the refectory are perfectly preserved together with the cellars and the 14th-century cloister, beside the remains of the abbey church and chapter house. The wooded setting beside the sea is

delightful. From here southwards to St. Quay-Portrieux the main road stays inland with side roads here and there, following wooded valleys to the sea. One such road leads to **Bréhec-en-Plouha**, a charming village in a little bay with a sandy beach, surrounded by unspoilt countryside. A few kilometres to the south is **Plage Bonaparte** from which during World War II a clandestine 'Channel bus service' carried shotdown Allied aircrews to freedom (see Box). **Plouha**, on a little river leading to the sea, provides opportunities for sea fishing in the *Marie-Georgette* (tel 96.20.30.93) and camping in the grounds of an old manor house, the Domaine de Keravel. The GR34 path which rambles around the entire northern coastline reaches a height of 100m at the tip of Plouha Point and affords a view right across the Gulf of St. Malo. A few kilometres inland is the 13th-century chapel of Kermaria-an-Iskuit with unique frescoes portraying a *danse macabre* in which the grim reaper sweeps up rich and poor alike.

St. Quay-Portrieux is the largest resort on the Côte du Goelo, so named after the Breton schooner which used to roam dangerous remote seas. Pleasure boats ply between here and the Bréhat 'isle of flowers', a voyage lasting 1½ hours. The town has several good sandy beaches and a casino and a selection of reasonably priced hotels. There are good facilities for tennis and golf, especially the latter. A new course in the 100-hectare grounds of the 12th-century Château de Coatguélen *en route* to Lanvollon was originally intended for the enjoyment of the family which owned it but the castle is now a hotel and the golf course, along with tennis courts, riding stables, an open

La Maison d'Alphonse

'*Bonjour à tous dans la maison d'Alphonse*' was the message crackling across the Channel from the BBC transmitters in England in 1944. It was the signal for the escape network (*réseaux d'évasion*) to marshal up to 25 Allied aircrew at a time at a cottage on the cliffs overlooking Cochat Cove in the Bay of St. Brieuc. These men had been shot down on raids over German-occupied Europe; many had escaped from PoW camps. They were hidden in the homes of the *hébergeurs*, in attics and barns, awaiting that signal and the arrival of a British corvette to pick them up from dinghies three or five kilometres offshore. They called it 'the Channel bus service'. The beach is today Plage Bonaparte after the codename of the operation and there is a granite monument on the cliff '*À la Gloire de Tous les Réseaux d'Evasion*'.

air swimming pool, a fishing lake and a children's play area are part of its facilities. There are 'golfing gourmet weekends' and cookery courses in the château's kitchens. A few kilometres to the south at **Lantic**, the 18-hole Ajoncs d'Or takes its name from the carpet of gorse which covers most of it, although there is also woodland and lakes making for an interesting game. It is owned by the municipality but the standards are as high as those on any private course. It is situated on the fringes of the Bois de-la-Salle, 7km to the west of St. Quay-Portrieux and a similar distance from **Étables-sur-Mer**, a lively, young resort on a plateau a kilometre or so inland with avenues leading to two sandy beaches. **Binic**, to the south, is another fishing village given over to holiday pleasures, with splendid views out to sea past the lighthouse and scenic drives and walks inland. Binic also boasts its own museum telling the story of the Newfoundland fishermen and the local folk arts and traditions. South-east, just beyond the Pointe de Pordic, is the beach of **Les Rosaires**, only a few kilometres from the centre of St. Brieuc.

St. Brieuc, capital of the Côtes-du-Nord, commands the promontory above two valleys, each spanned by great viaducts. The best views are from the tertre Aubé, tertre Notre-Dame or the Rondpoint Huguin, while the nearby Pointe du Roselier provides a panorama of the city in relation to the wide bay which takes its name.

One wonders what St. Brieuc (or Brioc) one of the original seven saints who landed here from Britain in the 6th century would make of his eponymous 20th-century settlement, with its expressways and airport. The motorway that slices through the city has relieved the old main road from Lamballe of a tide of traffic that was threatening to overwhelm pleasant villages such as **Yffiniac**. It is worth driving through in the summer when the villagers lay out their sacks of potatoes and strings of onions and garlic for sale at much lower prices than in town.

St. Brieuc's city fathers had the good sense as long ago as 1976 to ban the motor car from the old district of the place de la Grille and later from the

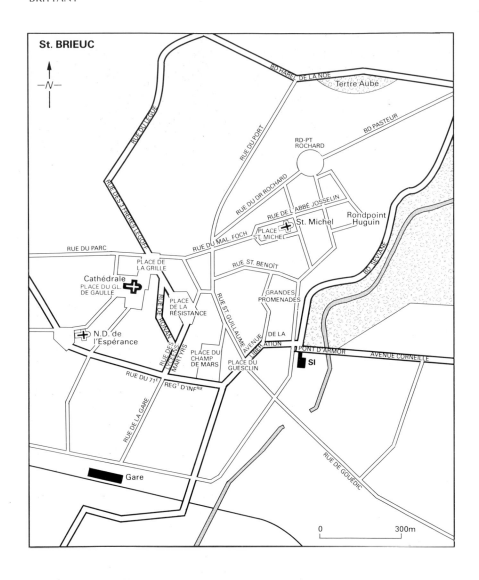

St. BRIEUC

—N—

BD HAREL DE LA NOE

Tertre Aubé

RUE DU LEGUE

RUE DU PORT

BD PASTEUR

RD-PT
ROCHARD

RUE DU DR ROCHARD

RUE DE L'ABBÉ JOSSELIN

RUE DES X FRÈRES LE GOFF

St. Michel

Rondpoint
Huguin

RUE DU MAL. FOCH

PLACE
ST MICHEL

RUE DU PARC

PLACE DE
LA GRILLE

RUE ST. BENOÎT

BD SÉVIGNÉ

Cathédrale
PLACE DU GL.
DE GAULLE

PLACE
DE LA
RÉSISTANCE

GRANDES
PROMENADES

N.D. de
l'Espérance

RUE ST GUILLAUME

RUE DES X/ MARTYRS

RUE DE CH...

PLACE DU
CHAMP
DE MARS

AVENUE DE LA

AVENUE DE LA LIBÉRATION

PONT D'ARMOR

AVENUE CORNEILLE

PLACE DU
GUESCLIN

SI

RUE DU 71E REGT D'INFERIE

RUE DE LA GARE

RUE DE GOUÉDIC

Gare

0   300m

lively 1980s shopping precinct, the place du Chai, even if this does create a drivers' nightmare in the surrounding streets. Somehow, it doesn't seem like a tourists' city, it is far too workaday and businesslike and lacks the visible historic attractions of, say, Dinan. The 12th- and 14th-century cathedral of St.

Étienne faces a glass and concrete Mairie and yet the blend of ancient and modern is skilful and seems to work. Development and restoration have gone hand in hand. The history of St. Brieuc is as colourful as most Breton towns from its foundation by the Welsh monk (St. Brieuc is now twinned with

Aberystwyth) through endless wars, sieges, famines and plagues. The present century brought its quota of conflict—during the German occupation the Resistance destroyed a fuel depot at St. Brieuc and seized the prison, releasing 32 *maquisards* who had been condemned to die by the Gestapo.

St. Brieuc is well provided with hotels (mostly on the outskirts), restaurants, crêperies, or if you are weary of those, elegant patisseries, department stores and antique shops, libraries, banks, garages, nightclubs, discothèques, travel agencies and much else. It has good communications by road, rail and air. It is, in short, an excellent base for exploring northern Brittany.

The Northern Argoat

Our circuit of Brittany's coast is now complete, but there remains one piece of unexplored territory, the northern part of the hinterland or Argoat. The call of the sea is always strong in Brittany but it is far from wise to miss the many treasures and half-secret places which lie along uncrowded inland roads, never more than a short drive from the better-known seaside resorts, harbours and beaches.

Travelling inland from Morlaix instead of looping around the Côte du Granit Rose, the N12 expressway delivers us rapidly to **Belle-Isle-en-Terre** the liltingly named gateway to the Coat an Noz (Wood of the Night) and Coat an Hay (Wood of the Day). There are two chapels worth visiting in the vicinity: Locmaria and Loc-Envel, both 15th-century and both endowed with spectacular rood screens. This is the mystical heart of the Argoat and a few

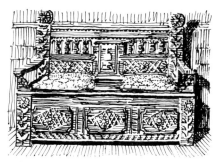

The banc-coffre (bench-cum-chest) is a traditional form of Breton furniture, often finely carved

kilometres east of Belle-Isle-en-Terre is the highest point in north Brittany, **Ménez-Bré**, a place where Druids and Christians have sent their prayers to heaven. At the crest with an uninterrupted view of the Monts d'Arrée to the west is the little stone chapel of St. Hervé, a monk and a bard who was also a horse thief and could cure head disorders, whether of the scalp or the brain. Moreover, he was blind from birth. After the saint came a priest known as Tadik-Coz (Little Old Father) who was known far and wide for his *offeren drantel* at Ménez-Bré, the last of thirty masses said for a dead man's soul to drive out demons. This final mass was said backwards to a congregation consisting of the souls of all those who had died in the neighbourhood in the previous year.

From Lannion, following the Léguer valley inland to Belle-Isle-en-Terre, there is a trail of chapels and châteaux to satisfy the most ardent of sightseers. **Kerfons** has a Renaissance chapel, **Tonquédec** castle with its twin courtyards and towers and ruined keep overlooking the valley beside a fast-flowing stream contrasts with the stylish château of Kergrist, combining several

La Tour d'Auvergne (1743—1800)

This Breton hero of the Napoleonic Wars, dubbed by Bonaparte 'Defender of the Fatherland and First Grenadier of the Armies of the Republic', was born in Carhaix to a local lawyer, Oliver-Louis Corret, and baptised Théophile-Malo. His father died when he was five and from his earliest years his dreams of military glory were encouraged by his mother but as a bourgeois, the doors of the École Militaire in Paris were closed to him. Instead, with the help of his uncle, a Jesuit father, he managed to get into the Black Musketeers of the King's Guard, which led to a commission as a sous-lieutenant in the Angoumois Regiment. It was impossible to rise very far in the army of the Ancien Régime without blue blood and Théophile-Malo discovered some in his own veins by way of an ancestress, Adèle Corret, who had been mistress of the Prince de la Tour d'Auvergne in the early 17th century. He was allowed to adopt this rather grander name than his own. Soon afterwards, now in his late thirties, he saw action for the first time.

Lieutenant de La Tour d'Auvergne distinguished himself brilliantly in a Franco-Spanish expedition to recapture the Balearic island of Minorca from the English. But he was reprimanded by the general commanding the French forces and recalled to France for not having obtained the permission of the Minister of War to go to Minorca in the first place. Kicking his heels in Strasbourg, he studied languages, painted and worked on a book on Celtic history. At 40 he became a captain, second class.

The Revolution transformed his prospects. La Tour d'Auvergne had no time either for his fellow-Breton anti-revolutionaries, the Chouans, or for his brother officers who emigrated rather than swear loyalty to the Constitution of the Republic. Regiments lost their names to numbers and he was given command of the grenadiers of the 80th Infantry, formerly the Angoumois. Fighting against the Austrians in the French Alps, he refused his right to a horse, giving the forage money to pay for two more foot soldiers from Finistère.

This was the genesis of the brave soldier with a cap of liberty and a haversack of books off to fight for the Republic portrayed in the painting *Le Départ de la Tour d'Auvergne* in the Musée des Beaux-Arts at Quimper. He reached 50 during the war against France's former ally, Spain, at Bayonne and sought leave to retire to his home town of Carhaix. But on his way to Brest he was shipwrecked and taken as a prisoner by the British Navy to Cornwall, where he felt quite at home, making notes on the similarities of speech for his book.

Exchanged for an English prisoner in France, he continued with his Celtic researches, but the army called and three times he returned to the colours, all the time dreaming of retirement to a manor house in the village of Trémargat, near Carhaix. He was embarrassed by Bonaparte's recognition of him as the First Grenadier, insisting that he was merely the *plus ancien*. He fell on 27 June 1800 from a lance thrust in action against the Austrians near Neuberg in Bavaria. Elaborate military ceremonies followed his death but his most lasting monument is his book *Origines Gauloises*.

architectural periods yet perfectly at home in its formal gardens reminiscent of Versailles, and finally the chapel of the Seven Saints near **Plouaret** is built around a megalith.

Guingamp, an old-fashioned greystone town on the banks of the River Trieux, is well placed for excursions in all directions. The spire and bell tower of the church, one Renaissance, its partner Gothic, overlook a classical fountain adorned with nymphs and dolphins. The basilica of Notre Dame-de-Bon-Secours is unusual and interesting. The north-west porch contains the famous 'Black Virgin' and on its floor a stone labyrinth with the inscription *Ave Maria* at its heart. The *pardon* takes place on the first Saturday in July and in August the town resounds to *bombarde*, *biniou* and the *danse du loup* (a stamping dance without music, originally to scare wolves away from the sheep) at an annual festival. By all accounts, in olden times the festival immediately followed the *pardon* and was the occasion for an uninhibited romp around the fountain in the place du Centre.

Guingamp is surrounded by beautiful woodlands, among them Coat Liou, d'Avaugour and Malaunay, with the River Trieux winding through them from its source further inland in the deepest Argoat, a territory of rocky gorges and lakes, dotted with chapels, calvaries and megalithic monuments, whose isolated villages and small towns have only recently seen more than the occasional tourist.

The now closed central section of the Canal de Nantes à Brest threads its way eastwards from Port de Carhaix to the lake of Guerlédan. **Carhaix-Plouguer**, just to the north of the canal, is a small town dominated by the statue of its most famous son, La Tour d'Auvergne, the 'First Grenadier' of Napoleon's army (see Box). Relics of the great man (buttons from his uniform, a lock of his hair) are kept under glass at the Mairie, rather like similar mementoes of Lord Nelson at Greenwich, and a festival is held annually in his honour. The town's origins go back to the Romans and in the 18th century it was at the centre of a thriving lead mining industry. A branch line of the railway runs from Carhaix to Guingamp by way of **Callac-de-Bretagne**, a favoured resort in Victorian times of the 'hunting, shooting and fishing' variety of Englishman. The streams are still full of fish and the wooded hills alive with game (although wolf and wild boar are extinct). Callac today is a sleepy little place with just one modestly priced restaurant, the Garnier, facing the station. The local calvary is said to have been erected on the spot where the Devil died from cold.

The heart of the green region lies to the east of Carhaix. Just beyond **Rostrenen**, a market town and site of a meteorological station, and **Gouarec**, a redundant canal port, on route N164 are the ruins of the 12th-century Abbey of Bon-Repos and a castle built by the Rohan family overlooking the lovely lakes of Fourneau and Salles with forest all around. The village of **St. Nicolas-du-Pélem** is worth visiting to see its ornate fountain incorporating a delicate Madonna. The heath to the north of the N164 is most dramatic—the aptly named **Chaos de Toul Goulic** is littered with rounded, moss-covered boulders as big as houses, beneath which rushes and roars the River Blavet, and the

155

Traditional ways: a fisherman paints his boat

Gorges du Daoulas through which the river of that name passes is only slightly less spectacular. Canal and rivers feed the huge man-made **Lake Guerledan**. In the midst of a green, undulating landscape, it covers 400 hectares offering wide scope for fishing and sailing and there is a 48km trekking path around it. **Mur-de-Bretagne** close by has become a popular resort but not to the extent of losing its traditional charm, although these are put in the shade by the neighbouring village of **St. Gilles-Vieux-Marché** whose houses, cottages and neat little auberges are smothered in flowers in summer.

Loudéac, at the edge of a forest in countryside rich in historical remains, chapels and calvaries, is well situated on the road to Rennes passing through the Forest of Hardouinais where Gilles de Bretagne was imprisoned and finally murdered.

In the direction of the northern coast there are other historic towns. **Quintin** on the River Gouet flowing down to St. Brieuc is still partly surrounded by the medieval ramparts which guarded the town and its streets are lined with 16th- and 17th-century half-timbered houses. It has a 17th-century château and its church contains a priceless relic, a piece of the Virgin's belt which is venerated by childless women. **Moncontour** is another little fortified granite town on a ridge at the meeting-point of two valleys. Its church has six beautifully worked 16th-century stained glass windows and faces a gracefully proportioned 18th-century square. Such gems are so thick on the ground in

FROM MORLAIX TO ST. BRIEUC

Brittany that it is all too easy to become blasé about them.

A few kilometres to the south of Moncontour is the tower of **Bel-Air** from which the green landscape unfolds to the distant horizons spanning Basse Bretagne, Haute Bretagne and the sea beyond. The peaceful country road and trekking path which wind hand in hand up the hill pass the chapel of Notre Dame-du-Haut, sometimes locked but if you can obtain the key from the nearby farm, what is inside is worth the effort. Here are seven vividly painted wooden statues: the healing saints of Brittany (*Sept Saints Guérisseurs*). St. Yverlin clasps his temple: he cures headaches. St. Mamert disposes of the colic. St. Lubin takes away rheumatic pains and doubles as an eye specialist. St. Méen deals with nervous disorders and St. Houarniaule (whom we met earlier under his alias, St. Hervé) calms irrational fears. That is why he holds a wolf on a lead—the sight of a werewolf was believed to induce a permanent state of the jitters. St. Hubert heals wounds, sores and rabies. The only female healing saint, Ste. Eugénie, comes to the aid of women in childbirth. One cannot help feeling that some at least of these saintly powers might be rather more helpful to tourists than 20th-century pills, but the best tonic after all is Brittany itself, with its marvellous heritage of faith and folklore.

BRITTANY

Part Three: Practical Information

Tourist offices (Offices de Tourisme and Syndicats d'Initiative)

CÔTES-DU-NORD—rue St. Goueno, 22000 St. Brieuc (96.33.32.50).

FINISTÈRE—34 rue Douarnenez, 29000 Quimper (98.53.72.72).

ILLE-ET-VILAINE—pont de Nemours, 35000 Rennes (99.79.01.98)

LOIRE-ATLANTIQUE—pl du Commerce, 44000 Nantes (40.47.04.51).

MORBIHAN—1 rue Thiers, 56000 Vannes (97.47.24.34).

These are the tourist offices in the main towns of each of the five Departments covered in this book. There are more than 200 such offices in towns large and small throughout the region, supplying detailed information to visitors about their own localities.

Recommended Hotels and Restaurants

A = Very Expensive, B = Expensive, C = Moderately Expensive, D = Moderate, E = Inexpensive—

L'ABER-WRAC'H: 29214 Finistère **Baie des Anges** (98.04.90.04). Relaxing family hotel with sea views. No restaurant. Rooms D-E.

AUDIERNE: 29113 Finistère **Le Goyen** (98.70.08.88). By the harbour, serves spectacular Belon oysters with caviare and grilled lobster á la cornouaillaise. Meals A-B. Rooms C-D (also 5 flats).
   Roi Gradlon (98.07.04.51). Beachside hotel with a reasonably priced menu. Meals B-E. Rooms D-E.

LA BAULE: 44500 Loire-Atlantique **Hermitage**, esplanade François-André (40.60.37.00). The pride of La Baule, set in its own pine-scented grounds facing the bay. Two restaurants, one on the beach. Meals A. Rooms A.
   Ty-Gwenn, 24 av Grande-Dune (40.60.37.07). Small but comfortable guesthouse (no restaurant) in a road leading to the beach in La Baule-les-Pins. Rooms D-E.

BEG-MEIL: 29170 Finistère **Thalamot** (98.94.97.38). Old-established family hotel serving local mullet, John Dory and shellfish. Meals B-D. Rooms C-E.

BELLE-ÎLE-EN-MER: 56360 Morbihan **Castel Clara**, Port Goulphar (97.31.84.21). Lovely garden on the cliffs that Sarah Bernhardt loved. Tables on terrace. Meals A-B. Rooms A.
   La Forge (restaurant) route Port Goulphar, Bangor (97.31.51.76).

BÉNODET: 29118 Finistère **Armoric**, 3 rue Penfoul (98.57.04.03). Twelve rooms have direct access to the garden for elderly and handicapped. No meals. Rooms (all with WC) D-E.

2.5km north-east at Clohars-Fouesnant **Domaine de Kereven** (98.57.02.46). Old manor in its own grounds with golf nearby. Meals C. Rooms C.

BREST: 29200 Finistère **Sofitel Oceania**, 82 rue Siam (98.80.66.66). Meals A-C. Rooms B-E.

Voyageurs, 15 av Clemenceau (98.80.25.73). Turbot and shellfish on a lavish scale. Grill more modest with wine by the carafe. (Closed 15 July to 7 August and Mondays.) Meals A-E. Rooms C-E.

BRIGNOGAN-PLAGES: 29238 Finistère **Castel Régis**, plage Garo (98.83.40.22). Beach facilities, garden, tennis and swimming pool. Meals A-B. Rooms B-D.

CALLAC: 22160 Côtes-du-Nord **Garnier** (96.45.50.09). Modest restaurant (with rooms) opposite the railway station. Meals B-E. Rooms E.

CAMARET: 29129 Finistère **de France** (98.27.93.06). Modern hotel in traditional style with paintings and tapestries. On the harbour side. Meals A-E. Rooms B-E.

CANCALE: 35260 Ille-et Vilaine **de Bricourt**, 1 rue du Guesclin (99.89.64.76). Two Michelin stars, garden and just six bedrooms. Meals A. Rooms A.

Le Cancalais, quai Gambetta (99.89.61.93). Good food, harbour views. Meals B-C. Rooms E.

Phare (restaurant) at the harbourside (99.89.60.24). A good place to taste the local oysters and other *fruits de mer* in style. Meals B-D. Rooms E.

Pointe du Grouin 4.5km N on D201 (33.89.60.55). Quiet little hotel with tremendous views of the bay of Mont St. Michel. Meals C-D. Rooms D-E.

Ti Breiz (restaurant), quai Gambetta (99.89.60.26). Comfortable harbourside place. Meals A-B.

CAP FRÉHEL: 22 Côtes-du-Nord **Relais de Fréhel** 2.5km from the lighthouse on D16. Isolated, peaceful spot with magnificent views near Fort La Latte. Meals D. Rooms E.

CARNAC: 56340 Morbihan **Novotel**, au Atlantique (97.52.53.54). Large by Brittany standards. Swimming pool, garden, special prices for children. Meals B-C. Rooms A-B.

CHÂTEAULIN: 29150 Finistère **Auberge Ducs du Lin** (98.86.04.20). Favourite hideaway of anglers, 1.5km south on old Quimper road. Lovely views. Meals A-C. Rooms D.

CHÂTEAUNEUF-DU-FAO: 29119 Finistère **Relais de Cornouaille**, route Carhaix (98.81.75.36). Plain but pleasing little hostelry. Meals C-E. Rooms E.

CONCARNEAU: 29110 Finistère **Le Galion** (restaurant), 15 rue St. Guénolé (98.97.30.16). Inside the 'Ville Close'. Try langoustines with asparagus or turbot in champagne. Meals A-B. Rooms (just five) B.

DINAN: 22100 Côtes-du-Nord **Hôtel d'Avaugour**, 1 pl du Champ Clos (96.39.07.49). Charming hotel in one of the two main squares, with excellent food. Meals A-B. Rooms C.

DINARD: 35800 Ille-et-Vilaine **Le Grand**, 46 av George V (99.46.10.28). A truly Grand Hotel with the Yacht Club and Casino on the doorstep. Half of the rooms have a view of the Baie de la Vicomte. Gastronomic restaurant. Meals B. Rooms A-B.

    Beauséjour pl du Calvaire (99.46.14.69). Rambling building, informal atmosphere, 300m from St. Énogat beach. Restaurant good value. Meals D. Rooms, some big enough for whole family, E.

    At **La Jouvente** (7km on D114 and D5)—**Manoir de la Rance** (99.88.53.76). Peaceful hideaway, ideal for fishing, boating, lovely river views. No restaurant. Rooms B-C.

DOUARNENEZ: 29100 Finistère **Bretagne**, 23 rue Duguay-Trouin (98.92.30.44). Good base for exploring port. No restaurant. Rooms E.

    5km south-east on Quimper road D765, **Auberge de Kereoc'h** (99.92.07.58). Refurbished farmhouse in a wood. Excellent food. Meals B-D. Rooms D-E.

ERDEVEN: 56410 Morbihan **Voyageurs**, rue de l'Océan (97.55.64.47). Homely family hotel, especially good value for children. Meals C-E. Rooms D-E.

    1km north-west on route Pont-Lorois, **Auberge du Sous-Bois** (97.55.66.10). Charming inn with a pretty garden. Meals C-E. Rooms D.

    1.5km north-east on D105, **Château de Kéravéon** (97.55.68.55). 18th-century castle in a private park. Meals A-B. Rooms A.

LE FAOU: 29142 Finistère **Vieille Renommée**, pl Mairie (98.81.90.31). Good traditional Breton fare. Meals A-D. Rooms D-E.

LA FORÊT-FOUESNANT: 29133 Finistère **Espérance**, pl Église (98.56.96.58). Close to ancient calvary. Quiet garden, a local favourite. Meals A-D. Rooms D-E.

    1.5km on D783, **Manoir du Stang** (98.56.97.37). Beautiful old house in lovely gardens less than 1km from the sea. Meals A-B. Rooms A.

FOUESNANT: 29170 Finistère **Armorique**, 33 rue de Cornouaille (98.56.00.19). Traditional Breton inn with courtyard. Rooms in modern annexe. Meals B-D. Rooms A-B.

FOUGÈRES: 35300 Ille-et-Vilaine **Voyageurs**, 10 pl Gambetta (99.99.08.20) restaurant (99.99.14.17). Two quite separate establishments sharing the same address and both highly recommended. Meals B-C. Rooms E.

GUIDEL-PLAGES: 56520 Morbihan **L'Auberge Cadieu** (97.05.98.39). Cheerful, relaxed family hotel with bright rooms and restaurant overlooking shore. Meals C-D. Rooms E.

GUILVINEC: 29115 Finistère **du Centre**, 16 rue Penmarc'h (98.58.10.44). Basic accommodation, impressive menu. Meals B-E. Rooms E.

GUINGAMP: 22200 Côtes-du-Nord **Relais du Roy**, pl du Centre (96.43.76.62). Louis XIII dined here. Still has fine cuisine served on Limoges ware, plus seven comfortable rooms all with baths. Meals A-B. Rooms A-C.

HENNEBONT: 56700 Morbihan, 4km south on D781 **Château de Locguénolé** and **Résidence de Kernavien** (97.76.29.04). In a park on the banks of the Blavet. Swimming, tennis, superb food. Meals A-B. Rooms A-B.

JOSSELIN: 56120 Morbihan **Château**, 1 rue Général de Gaulle (97.22.20.11). Conveniently situated with a fine view of the castle. Meals B-E. Rooms E.

LAMBALLE: 22400 Côtes-du-Nord **La Tour d'Argent**, 2 rue du Lavergne (96.31.01.37). Good value relais with separate dining room (500m). Meals B-E. Rooms D-E.

    3.5km at hamlet of La Poterie via D28 **Auberge du Manoir des Portes** (96.31.13.62). Converted from a 15th-century fortified farmhouse and courtyard, with sauna, swimming, tennis, fishing and riding. Meals A-C. Rooms A.

LAMPAUL-PLOUARZEL: 29229 Finistère **Auberge du Kruguel** (98.84.01.66). Salmon like you've never tasted it before. Meals A-B. No accommodation.

LANNION: 22300 Côtes-du-Nord **Le Serpolet** (restaurant), 1 rue F. le Dantec (96.46.50.23). Food prepared with flair, wide range of menus, wine by carafe if required. Meals A-D.

LOCMARIAQUER: 56740 Morbihan **L'Escale** (97.57.32.51). Modern building in Breton style with steep pitched slate roof. Harbourside terrace. meals C-D. Rooms D-E.

LOCQUIREC: 29241 Finistère **Port** (98.67.42.10). Family-run harbourside hotel. Basic accommodation, sea views. Meals A-D. Rooms C-E.

LOCRONAN: 29136 Finistère **Fer à Cheval** (restaurant) pl Église (98.91.70.74). Huge portions of tasty seafood. Hotel of same name, modern in trad. style, 1km south-east on D63 (98.91.70.67. Meals A-E. Rooms D-E.

    3km northwest on C10, **Manoir de Moellian** (98.92.50.40). In clement weather meals served outdoors in lovely gardens of 17th-century stone building. Meals A-D. Rooms B-D.

MISSILLAC: 44160 Loire-Atlantique **Golf de la Bretesche** (40.88.30.05). Peaceful country surroundings with golf, tennis, swimming in the setting of a beautiful château. Meals A-C. Rooms C-D.

    Parc de la Brière (40.88.30.12). Modest country lodge with comfortable rooms and good food. Meals D-E. Rooms D-E.

MOËLAN-SUR-MER: 29116 Finistère, 2km north west, **Le Moulins du Duc** (98.39.60.73). Converted from historic buildings in a green setting. Indoor pool. Meals A-B. Rooms A-B.

LE MONT ST. MICHEL: 50116 Manache **Mère Poulard** (33.60.14.01). Inside the island fortress. Norman and Breton dishes as well as the famous omelette. Plain but expensive accommodation. Meals A-C. Rooms A.

At **La Digue**, 2km south on D976, **St. Aubert** (33.60.08.74). A pleasant hotel with a swimming pool, a garden and outdoor service. Meals C-E. Rooms D-E.

MORGAT: 29160 Finistère **Julia** (98.27.05.89). Quiet, with its own garden. Low priced menu for kids. Meals B-E. Rooms D-E.

Le Roof (restaurant), bd France Libre (98.27.08.40). The best in town for fresh seafood. Meals A-E.

MORLAIX: 29210 Finistère **Europe**, 1 rue Aiguillon (98.62.11.99). Largish hotel, varied menu of seafood and crêpes. Well-stocked cellar. Meals A-D. Rooms C-E.

MUZILLAC: 56190 Morbihan **Auberge de Pen-Mur**, 20 route Vannes (97.41.67.58). Just off N165, a good stopover or place to enjoy an excellent meal at a moderate price. Meals C-E. Rooms D-E.

At **Billiers** (2.5km S on D5) **Glycines**, pl Église (97.41.64.63). Modest little inn with a garden and rooms with private showers and toilets. Meals C-E. Rooms E.

NANTES: 44000 Loire-Atlantique **La Cigale** (restaurant), 4 place Graslin (40.69.76.41). A brasserie in early 1900s style. Good value. Meals C-E.

Les Maraîchers (restaurant), 21 rue Fouré (40.47.06.51). Exquisite food and local wines. Booking essential. Meals A.

Le Colvert (restaurant), 14 rue Armand-Brossard (40.48.20.02). Not the smartest but certainly one of the best value places to eat in Nantes. Meals D.

At **Orvault** (7km on N137 and D42), **Domaine d'Orvault** (40.76.84.02). A country estate providing luxurious accommodation, gourmet menus and the finest Muscadet and Anjou wines. Meals A-C. Rooms A-B.

PAIMPOL: 22500 Côtes-du-Nord **Le Repaire de Kerroc'h**, 22 quai Morand (96.20.50.13). Late 18th-century quayside mansion. Varied and interesting menu. Meals A-D. Rooms D-E.

At **Lanvollon**, 11km on D7, **Château de Coatguelen** (96.22.31.24). Private golf course, swimming and tennis. Gourmet food. Meals A. Rooms A-B.

PEILLAC: 56 Morbihan **Chez Antoine** (99.91.24.43). Attractive inn with parking at the door and a pretty garden. Chef-proprietor produces varied menu. Meals B-E. Rooms E.

PERROS-GUIREC: 22700 Côtes-du-Nord **Printania**, 12 rue Bons Enfants (96.23.21.00). Sea views, garden and tennis. Meals A-B. Rooms A-B.

Cyrnos, 10 rue Sergent L'Heveder (96.23.20.42). Peaceful hideaway. No restaurant. Rooms E.

PLÉNEUF-VAL-ANDRÉ: 22370 côtes-du-Nord **Le Biniou** (restaurant), 121 rue Clemenceau (96.72.24.35). Friendly astmosphere, good regional cuisine. Meals D-E.
At the **port de Plegu** (1km) **Cotriade** (restaurant) (96.72.20.26). Michelin star for its fine cooking, especially lobster and other shellfish, also fillets of sole in saffron butter. But be warned, places are limited and advance booking essential. Meals A-B.

POINTE DU RAZ: 29113 Finistère **Baie des Trépassés** (98.70.61.34). An oasis of peace 3,5km from the 'pointe du razzamatazz'. Quiet garden in which to contemplate views. Meals A-D. Rooms D-E.

PONT-AVEN: 29123 Finistère **Moulin de Rosmadec** (restaurant). By a bridge in the town centre, terrace on the river. Superb lobster, white fish and duck. Meals A-C.

PONTIVY: 56300 Morbihan **Le Villeneuve**, on the Vannes road (97.39.83.10). A logis well recommended for regional cuisine. Meals C-E. Rooms E.

POULDREUZIC: 29143 Finistère, 3km along road to Audierne, **Moulin de Brenizenec** (98.91.30.33). Old mill converted to a comfortable hotel in a landscaped garden. No restaurant. Rooms B-C.

LE POULDU: 29121 Finistère **Armen** (98.39.90.44). Good family hotel with its own garden. Meals B-E. Rooms C-E.

QUESTEMBERT: 56230 Morbihan **Bretagne** (restaurant), rue St. Michel (97.26.11.12). Not so much a place to eat as a gastronomic experience with caviare and truffles blended with Breton seafood and Muscadet wines. Booking essential. Six bedrooms. Meals A-B. Rooms A.

QUIBERON: 56170 Morbihan **Sofitel** (97.50.20.00). A thalassotherapy centre with the best of locations, restful garden, tennis and swimming. Meals A-B. Rooms A.

QUIMPER: 29000 Finistère **Tour d'Auvergne**, 12 rue Reguaires (98.95.08.70). Old style Breton décor and cooking. Meals B-D. Rooms C-E,
    Capucin Gourmand (restaurant), 29 rue Reguaires (98.95.43.12). Highly rated for inventive menus. Meals B-C.
    3km along the road to Bénodet, **Griffon** and **Creach Gwenn** (restaurant) (98.90.33.33). Pleasant surroundings of a well-kept garden, indoor swimming pool. Meals A-D. Rooms C-D.

QUIMPERLÉ: 29130 Finistère, 2km south on D49, **Ermitage** (98.96.04.66). Restful little hotel in its own grounds, with swimming pool. Meals C-D. Rooms C-D.

QUINTIN: 22800 Côtes-du-Nord **du Commerce**, 2 rue Rochonen (96.74.94.67). Good, old-fashioned country hotel serving delicious local pâtés, coq au vin, seafood and rich desserts. Meals B-E. Rooms E.

REDON: 35600 Ille-et-Vilaine **Jean-Marc Chandouineau**, 10 av Gare (99.71.02.04). A very comfortable place to take a break from sightseeing, with just five bedrooms for those wishing to extend their stay. Meals B-D. Rooms C-E.

RENNES: 35000 Ille-et-Vilaine **Palais** (restaurant), 7 pl Parlement de Bretagne (99.79.45.01) has very special ways of serving oysters and rabbit. Meals B-C.

RIEC-SUR-BÉLON: 29124 Finistère **Chez Mélanie** (restaurant), facing the church (98.06.91.05). Superb cooking, some basic accommodation. Meals A-C. Rooms E.

LA ROCHE-BERNARD: 56130 Morbihan **Deux Magots** (99.90.60.75). Quiet, comfortable small hotel with a very good low-priced menu. Meals C-E. Rooms C-E.
  Auberge Bretonne, 2 pl du Guesclin (99.90.60.28). An old house that used to be a *crêperie*. Young chef produces food of a high quality. A few simple bedrooms. Meals B-C. Rooms E.

ROSCOFF: 29211 Finistère **Gulf Stream**, rue Marquise de Kergariou (98.69.73.19). Pleasant hotel with sea views, garden and swimming pool. Meals A-B. Rooms B-C.

SABLES-D'OR-LES-PINS: 22 Côtes-du-Nord **Diane** (96.41.42.07) Three minutes' walk to the beach, pleasant gardens, terraces for meals and balconies to many rooms. No restaurant. Rooms D-E.
  At **Vieux Bourg de Pléhérel** (3.5km on D34) **Plage et Fréhal**. Neat, simple hotel in a quiet situation with extensive views. Short walk to the beach. Good food and service. Meals C-E. Rooms E.

ST. CAST-LE-GUILDO: 22380 Côtes-du-Nord **Angleterre et Panorama**, rue Fosserole (96.41.91.44). Built in the style of a classical Italian villa, amidst pine trees in its own gardens. Sunny terraces on each floor with charming views. Meals C-D. Rooms E.
  At the adjoining beach area of Pen-Guen, **Le Biniou** (restaurant) (96.41.94.53). Famed for its good food, including many Breton seafood specialities. Meals A-D, but the cheaper menus are excellent value.

ST. GUÉNOLÉ: 29132 Finistère **Sterenn** (98.58.60.36). A small family hotel on the Eckmühl road with a striking view of the Pointe de Penmarc'h. Meals A-D. Rooms C-D.

ST. MALO: 35400 Ille-et-Vilaine INTRA-MUROS **Duchesse Anne** (restaurant), 5 pl Guy La Chambre (99.40.85.33). Built almost into the ramparts. Michelin star. Try lobster, foie gras frais de canard, or Tarte Tatin (upside-down apple tart). Meals A-B.
  Noguette, 9 rue Foss (99.40.83.57). Nice little hotel next to the central market. Cheaper menu good. Meals D-E. Rooms D-E.

ST. MARC-SUR-MER: 44600 Loire-Atlantique **La Plage** (40.91.99.01). Quiet hotel on the beach famed as the setting for *Monsieur Hulot's Holiday*. Rooms with private baths and showers, sea views. Meals C-E. Rooms E.

ST. QUAY-PORTRIEUX: 22410 Côtes-du-Nord **Ker Mor** 13 rue Pt le Senecal (96.70.52.22). Quiet garden, sea views. Private tennis. Meals A-D. Rooms B-C.

ST. THÉGONNEC: 29223 Finistère **Auberge St. Thégonnec**, 6 pl Marie (98.79.61.18). Simple village inn serving fresh local produce, well prepared. Pleasant garden. Meals A-D. Rooms (six only) C-E.

STE. ANNE-LA-PALUD: 29127 Finistère **Plage** (98.92.50.12). Superior hotel beside the beach and dunes with a garden, tennis and swimming pool, plus gourmet food. Meals A. Rooms A.

STE. MARINE: 29120 Finistère **Le Jeanne d'Arc** (restaurant) (98.56.32.70). Deservedly praised for exquisite seafood. Very much in demand. Meals A-B. Rooms (limited) E.

TINTÉNIAC: 35190 Ille-et-Vilaine **Voyageurs** (99.68.02.21) is a small cosy inn near the canal, renowned for good value and good food. Meals B-E. Rooms D-E.

TRÉBEURDEN: 22560 Côtes-du-Nord **Ti al-Lannec** (96.23.57.26). Granite manor in its own grounds with sea views. Relais du Silence but children are welcomed. Meals A-B. Rooms A-C.

TRÉGASTEL-PLAGE: 22730 Côtes-du-Nord **Grève Blanche** (96.23.88.27). Quiet. Sea views. Modestly priced accommodation. Meals A-B. Rooms C-E.

TRÉGUIER: 22220 Côtes-du-Nord **Estuaire**, pl Général de Gaulle (96.92.30.25). No frills accommodation, good food in dining room overlooking the quay. Meals B-D. Rooms E.
2km south-west on road to Lannion, **Kastell Dinec'h** (96.92.49.39). Peaceful old house among the flowerbeds. Meals A-C. Rooms B-E.

TRÉVOU-TRÉGUIGNEC: 22660 Côtes-du-Nord **Ker Bugalic** (96.23.72.15) Meals A-D. rooms D-E.
Tréstel-Bellevue (93.23.71.44). Meals B-C. Rooms E. Both are quiet hotels with gardens and nice views. The latter applies a no-smoking rule to its bedrooms.

LA TRINITÉ-SUR-MER: 56470 Morbihan **Les Hortensias** (97.55.73.69). Gourmet restaurant in a delightful garden setting on a hill overlooking the yacht marina. Meals A.

VANNES: 56000 Morbihan **Manche Océan**, 31 rue Lt-Col Maury (97.47.26.46). Comfortable larger hotel, centrally placed, but no restaurant. Rooms C-D.
Marebaudière, 4 rue A. Briand (97.47.34.29). Modestly priced yet comfortable. Rooms D-E.
At **Conleau** 4.5km south-west, **Le Roof** (97.63.47.47). Nice terrace and dining room with wide views. Meals A-D. Rooms C-E.

VITRÉ: 35500 Ille-et-Vilaine **Petit-Billot**, 5 pl Mar.-Leclerc (99.75.02.10). Nice, homely little hotel with a reputation for good food at moderate prices. Meals C-E. Rooms E.

Events

BELZ (Morhiban): 3rd Sunday in September, Pardon of St. Cado, who came from Wales.

BUEZEC-CAP SIZUN (Finistère): 2nd Sunday of August, Fête of the Bruyères (heather).

BULAT-PESTIVIEN (Côtes-du-Nord): 2nd Sunday in September, Pardon de Notre-Dame-de-Bulat.

CARNAC (Morbihan): 3rd Sunday in August, Grande Fête de Menhirs; 2nd Sunday in September, cattle festival of St. Cornély (Cornelius) patron saint of Carnac.

CHÂTEAUNEUF-DU-FAO (Finistère): 15 August, international festival of folk dancing (de danses et traditions populaires).

CONCARNEAU (Finistère): 3rd Sunday in August, fishermen's festival of blessing the blue nets (Fête des Filets Bleus).

DINARD (Ille-et-Vilaine): July—International Tennis and Volley Ball Tournaments. August—Académie Internationale of music and dance, two separate festivals. International Show Jumping Competition. Pardon de la Mer. June to September—Spectacle d'ambiance (lights and music).

LE FAOUET (Morbihan): End of June, Pardon of Ste. Barbe (St. Barbara); last Sunday in August, Pardon of St. Fiacre.

LE FOLGOËT (Finistère): 1st Sunday in September, Pardon of Notre-Dame at the famous shrine of 'the Fool in the Wood'.

FOUESNANT (Finistère): 3rd Sunday of July—Fête des Pommiers, the festival of the cider makers.

FOUGÈRES (Ille-et-Vilaine): end of August to beginning of September, Festival du Livre Vivant, drama, pageants, floodlit spectacle.

GUENIN (Morbihan): end of July, Procession of Notre-Dame du Mene-Guen.

GUINGAMP (Côtes-du-Nord): 1st Sunday in July, Pardon of Notre-Dame de Bon-Secours; mid-August Festival of Breton dance.

HÉDÉ (Ille-et-Vilaine): in mid-August this little town holds its own festival of arts and history around its ruined castle on a ridge.

JOSSELIN (Morbihan): 2nd Sunday in September, Procession of Notre-Dame-du-Roncier.

KÉRITY-PAIMPOL (Côtes-du-Nord): 28 May, Pardon of Ste. Barbe (St. Barbara).

LAMBALLE (Côtes-du-Nord): 2nd Sunday in July, Folklore Festival of the Ajoncs d'Or (golden gorse).

168

LIZIO (Morbihan): Mid-August, Festival des Artisans, the working folk.

LOCRONAN (Finistère): 2nd Sunday in July, the Tromenie, religious procession.

LORIENT (Morbihan): 1st fortnight of August, international Celtic arts festival.

MORLAIX (Finistère): July and August, the Wednesday fêtes (Les Mercredis de Morlaix).

NANTES (Loire-Atlantique): early July, the Nantes Fête, arts, carnival.

PAIMPOL (Côtes-du-Nord): mid-July, Fêtes of Newfoundland and Iceland celebrate the historic connection of this port with distant fishing grounds.

PERROS-GUIREC (Côtes-du-Nord): 15 August, Pardon of Notre-Dame de la Clarté; 16 August, Fêtes of the hortensias.

PLONÉVEZ-PORZAY (Finistère): last Sunday in August, Pardon of St. Anne La Palud, subject of a famous poem (by Tristan Corbière) and painting (by Charles Cottet, Musée des Beaux-Arts, Rennes).

PLOUHA (Côtes-du-Nord): 3rd Sunday in September, Pardon of Kermaria-en-Isquit.

PLOMODIERN (Finistère): 15th August, Fêtes du Ménéz-Hom, the mountain which overshadows the village. Procession and pageant.

PONT-AVEN (Finistère): 1st Sunday of August, Fête of the Ajoncs d'Or (golden gorse).

PONT-CROIX (Finistère): 15 August, Pardon of Notre-Dame de Roscudon.

PONTIVY (Morbihan): 3rd Sunday in September, Pardon of Notre-Dame de la Joie.

QUITIN (Côtes-du-Nord): 2nd Sunday of May, Pardon of Notre-Dame de Délivrance.

QUIMPER (Finistère): last week in July, Festival de Cornouaille, plays in Breton, folk music, dancing, grand procession. Enthronement of Queen of Cornouaille.

QUIMPERLÉ (Finistère): Whitsun, Fête de Toulfouen.

REDON (Ille-et-Vilaine): mid-July to mid-August, the Festival of the Abbey, theatre, music, dance.

RENNES (Ille-et-Vilaine): end of June and beginning of July, night-time concerts and tableaux 'Les Tombées de la Nuit—Création Bretonne'.

ROCHEFORT-EN-TERRE (Morbihan): Sunday after 15 August, Pardon of Notre-Dame de la Tronchaye.

RUMENGOL (Finistère): Sunday after Pentecost (Whitsun), Pardon of Notre-Dame de Rumengol.

ST. BRIAC (Ille-et-Vilaine): 2nd Sunday in August, Fêtes des Mouettes (seagulls) with a procession of Breton dancers and pipe bands and Fest-Noz (night festival).

ST. BRIEUC (Côtes-du-Nord): May, Le Mai Breton folkloric festival; last weekend in May, Pardon of Notre-Dame de l'Espérance.

ST. GUÉNOLÉ-PENMARC'H (Finistère): 15 August, Pardon of Notre-Dame de la Joie.

ST. JEAN-TROMILON (Finistère): 3rd Sunday in September, Pardon of Notre-Dame Tronoen.

ST. QUAY-PORTRIEUX (Côtes-du-Nord): end of July, Pardon of Ste. Anne.

ST. MALO (Ille-et-Vilaine): July, Fêtes du Clos-Poulet; beginning of August, Festival of Sacred Music.

STE. ANNE D'AURAY (Morbihan): 25 and 26 July, Pardon of Ste. Anne, mother of the Virgin Mary and patroness of Brittany. With Le Folgoët, the greatest pardon of all.

TRÉGUIER (Côtes-du-Nord): end of May, Pardon of St. Yves, the lawyers' patron.

TRÉGUNC (Finistère): last Sunday in August, Pardon of St. Philibert.

LA TRINITÉ-PORHOËT (Morbihan): Pentecost (Whitsun), Pardon of La Trinité.

VANNES (Morbihan): 15 August, Grandes Fêtes d'Arvor, carnival, music, processions.

LE VIEUX-MARCHÉ (Côtes-du-Nord): end of July, Pilgrimage to the Chapel of the Seven Saints (the founders).

(This is a selection, not a complete list of all *pardons* and festivals in Brittany. Fuller details are kept by the Tourist Offices.)

Châteaux and Museums

Open 'daily' means morning and afternoon. Most open at 10am, shut for lunch (usually 12-2pm). Afternoon closing times vary according to season (usually 5 or 6pm). Most museums in France are closed on Tuesdays.

Châteaux

ALLAIRE-BÉGANNE (Morbihan) 16th-c. **Château Estier** (99.91.81.14). *Daily from 1 June to 15 Sept from 2-6pm.*

ANCENIS (Loire-Atlantique) **Château** (40.83.07.44). Daily July and Aug. *Guided tours 2-6pm except Mon.*

ANTRAIN-SUR-COUESNON (Ille-et-Vilaine) 11th-c. **Château Bonnefontaine** (99.98.31.13). *Daily from 5 Apr to 30 Sept.*

BASSE-GOULAINE (Loire-Atlantique) **Château de Goulaine** (40.54.91.42). Marquise de Goulaine and family in residence. Aviary of living tropical butterflies. *Daily 16 June to 15 Sept, 2-6.30pm, except Tue. Low season on weekends and bank holidays.*

BAZOUGES-LA-PÉROUSE (Ille-et-Vilaine) **Château La Balue** (99.97.44.11). Gardens and history of gardens in pictures. *Daily from 1 June to 1 Oct, 11am-12noon, 2.30-7pm.*

BÉCHEREL (Ille-et-Vilaine) **Château Caradeuc** (99.66.77.66). *Daily. Park open throughout the year from 8.30am to sunset.*

BIGAN (Morbihan) **Château Kerguehennec** (97.60.21.19). Park has fine collection of trees and sculptures. Centre of Contemporary Art. *Daily, year round.*

CHÂTEAUGIRON (Ille-et-Vilaine) **Château** (99.00.41.69).

CLÉDER (Finistère) **Château Tronjoly** (98.69.40.01). *Visits to outside only, on request.*

CLISSON (Loire-Atlantique) **Château** (40.78.02.22). *Daily year round, except Tue. Sound-and-light show inside the castle Fri and Sat during summer.*

COMBOURG (Ille-et-Vilaine) **Château**, birthplace of Chateaubriand (99.73.22.95). *Daily from 1 Mar to 30 Nov for the park, castle 2-5.30pm only.*

ELVEN (Morbihan) ruined **Château** (97.53.52.79).

ERQUY (Côtes-du-Nord) **Château Bienassis** (96.72.22.03). *Daily from 8 June to 15 Sept.*

FOUGÈRES (Ille-et-Vilaine) **Château** (99.99.05.48). *Daily Feb to Nov.*

FRÉHEL (Côtes-du-Nord) **Fort La Latte** (96.41.40.31). *Daily from 1 June to 20 Sept and weekends and bank holidays in May.*

171

LE GUERNO (Morbihan) **Château Branfére** and wildlife park (97.42.94.66). *Daily 30 Mar to 11 Nov.*

LES IFFS (Ille-et-Vilaine) **Château Montmuran** where du Guesclin was knighted and married (99.45.88.61). *Every afternoon from Easter to 1 Nov and on Sat and Sun afternoons in winter.*

JOSSELIN (Morbihan) **Château de Rohan** (97.22.22.50). *From 30 Mar to 1 June afternoons only Wed, Sun and bank holidays. In June and from 1-23 Sept daily, afternoons only. Daily from 1 July to 31 Aug.*

LANVELLEC (Côtes-du-Nord) 14th-c. **Château Rosanbo** (96.35.18.77). *Daily in peak season and 2-6pm from Easter to the end of June.*

LOCTUDY (Finistère) **Château Kerazan** (98.87.40.40). Open to visitors all year on request. *Daily from 15 June to 15 Sept. Closed on Tue.*

MONCONTOUR (Côtes-du-Nord) **Château La Touche-Trébry** (96.42.78.55). *Daily 1 July to 31 Aug, except Sun.*

MONTAUBAN-DE-BRETAGNE (Ille-et-Vilaine) feudal **Château** (99.06.40.21). *Daily 15 July to 30 Sept, 2-6pm.*

MOULINS (Ille-et-Vilaine) 18th-c. **Château Monbouan** (99.49.01.51). *Daily 15 July to 1 Sept.*

NANTES (Loire-Atlantique) **Château** (40.47.18.15). *Daily year round, except Tue.*

PONTIVY (Morbihan) **Château de Rohan** (97.25.12.93). *Daily 15 June to 30 Sept.*

PLÉDÉLIAC (Côtes-du-Nord) **Château la Hunaudaye** (96.31.61.05). *Daily, July and Aug. From Easter to 30 June and in Sept Sun only 3-7pm.*

PLEUGUENEUC (Ille-et-Vilaine) **Château Bourbansais** with park and zoo (99.45.20.42). *Daily year round.*

PLOMELIN (Finistère) Château de Perrenou *(98.94.22.72). Wed and Sun from 1 June to 30 Sept, 10am-12noon and 2-6pm.*

PLOUASNE (Côtes-du-Nord) **Château Caradeuc**, the Breton Versailles. *Daily.* No phone calls.

PLOUBEZRE (Côtes-du-Nord) **Château Kergrist** (96.38.91.44). *Daily in season, 2-6pm.*

PLOUZÉVÉDÉ (Finistère) **Château Kerjean** (98.69.93.69). *Daily, except Tue and bank holidays. Tours in French, English and German. Finistère manifestation—weekly show during summer.*

PONTRIEUX (Côtes-du-Nord) **Château la Roche-Jagu** (96.95.62.35). Cultural Meeting Centre, *open all year. Guided visits from 1 Apr to 15 Sept.*

QUINTIN (Côtes-du-Nord) two **Châteaux** in same park, 17th and 18th-c. (96.74.94.79). *Daily.*

ROCHEFORT-EN-TERRE (Morbihan) **Château** (97.43.31.78). *Daily Apr to Sept.*

ST. FLORENT-LE-VIEIL (Loire-Atlantique) at La Chapelle **Château la Baronnière** (41.78.53.49). *Daily from May to 15 Sept, except Tues.* Wines grown on the estate can be tasted free in the 16th-c. bakery.

ST. GOAZEC (Finistère) **Château Trévarez** (98.81.74.95). *Daily, in season.* Gardens especially beautiful May-June.

ST. MALO (Ille-et-Vilaine) **Château** (99.40.97.73). *Daily.*
   Limoelou Manor, home of Jacques Cartier (99.40.97.73) at Rothéneuf, *Daily 1 June to 30 Sept except Mon and Tue.*

ST. POL-DE-LÉON (Finistère) **Château Kerouzere** (98.29.96.05). *All year on request to owner M. de Calan.*

SARZEAU (Morbihan) **Château de Suscinio** (97.41.82.37). *Daily from 1 Apr to 30 Sept except Wed mornings. Rest of the year open on Tue, weekends and bank holidays.*
   Château de Kerlevenan (97.26.41.10) 17th-c. Italian style. *Open on request 1 July to 15 Sept 2-6pm.*

TONQUEDEC (Côtes-du-Nord) **Château.** *Daily.* No phone calls.

VITRÉ (Ille-et-Vilaine) Château *(99.75.04.54). Daily, year round.*
   Château les Rocher-Sévigné (99.96.61.96). *Daily.*
   Musée Tour St Laurent, inside the castle (99.75.04.54). *Daily. Closed Tue out of July-Sept peak.*

Museums

AUDIERNE (Finistère) **Les Grands Viviers** aquarium of shellfish, route de la Plage (98.70.10.04). *Daily in July and Aug.*
   La Chaumière, 5 rue Amiral-Guépratte (98.70.12.20) traditional Breton cottage.
   Pointe du Raz Museum, Plogoff (98.70.65.28). Reproduction of calvaries. *Daily.*

BAGUER-MORVAN (Ille-et-Vilaine) **Museum of Peasantry** (99.48.04.04). Agricultural implements. *Daily 1 May to 30 Sept.*

BELLE-ÎLE-EN-MER (Morbihan) **Le Palais** (97.31.84.17). *All year.*

BINIC (Côtes-du-Nord) **Local History and Marine.** *Afternoons and evenings from 1 June to 30 Sept.*

BRASPARTS (Finistère) **La Ferme St. Michel.** Craftworkers. *Daily, except Tue.*

BRECH-AURAY (Morbihan) **Ecomuseum** (97.24.22.24). *Year round.*

BREST (Finistère) **Municipal**, rue de la Traverse (98.44.66.27). *Daily except Tue.*
Marine, in the château (98.22.10.80). *Year round. Closed Tue.*
Motte-Tanguy Tower (98.45.05.31). (Brest harbour, fortifications and penal colony). *Year round.*

CAMARET (Finistère) **Naval**, Tour Vauban (98.27.91.12). *Daily, July to Sept.*

CARNAC (Morbihan) **Prehistoric: Miln le Rouzic** (97.52.22.04). *Year round.*
Tumulus St. Michel, *end of Mar to end of Sept.*

LA CHÈZE (Côtes-du-Nord) **Crafts** (96.26.63.16). Harness, cartwheels, sabots, anvils. Video films of current crafts. *Daily 1 June to 15 Sept. Out of season closed mornings and Mon.*

COMMANA (Finistère) **Ecomuseum of Monts d'Arrée**, Moulin de Kerouat (98.68.87.76). Traditional village with watermills. *Year round.*

CONCARNEAU (Finistère) **Fishing**, Ville Close (98.97.10.20). *Year round, to 8pm in summer.*
Minarium, Collège de France (98.97.06.59). Marine flora, fauna. *Daily in season.*

DINAN (Côtes-du-Nord) **Château de Duchesse Anne** (96.39.45.20). *Daily, year round. Closed Tue except in high season (June-Aug).*

DINARD (Ille-et-Vilaine) **Sea aquarium** (99.46.13.90). *Daily from Whitsun to September.*
Museum Villa Eugénie, 12 rue des Français-Libres (99.46.13.90). *Daily, Easter to 15 Nov.*

DOL-DE-BRETAGNE (Ille-et-Vilaine) **la Guillotière Manor**. History of Dol from St. Samson to Chateaubriand. *Daily, except Tue, from Easter to 30 Sept.*

DOUARNENEZ (Finistère) **Boat Museum**, pl de l'Enfer, Port Rhu (98.92.18.18). *Daily June to Sept. Out of season, by appointment.*

FOUGÈRES (Ille-et-Vilaine) **Shoe Museum** in Château (99.99.18.98). *Mar to Oct.*
De La Villeon life of local artist, impressionism (99.99.18.98). *Daily 1 July to 15 Sept. Out of season, weekends only.*

GUER (Morbihan) **St. Cyr Coetquidan** military museum at the Sandhurst of France (97.75.75.75). *Daily, year round.*

JOSSELIN (Morbihan) **Rohan Collection of Dolls** in the Château (97.22.36.45). *Daily 1 May to 30 Sept, except Mon. Out of season, Wed, weekends and bank holidays.*

LAMBALLE (Côtes-du-Nord) **Mathurin Meheut**, Breton painter (96.31.19.99). *Open daily 1 June to 15 Sept, except Sun and bank holidays.*
Folk Arts (96.31.05.38). *Same opening as Meheut Museum.*

LOCRONAN (Finistère) **Folk Arts and Traditions** (98.91.70.05). *Daily 15 June to 30 Sept. Out of season, by appointment.*

LORIENT (Morbihan) **Compagnie des Indes**. *Daily except Tuesdays. Closed 15 Nov to 15 Dec and 1 May.*
   De la Mer. *Daily, except Tue.*

MORLAIX (Finistère) **Jacobins**, 1 rue des Vignes (98.88.68.88). *Daily, all year, except Mon and Tue. Shut Mon only in peak season.*

NANTES (Loire-Atlantique) **d'Art Populaire Régional** and **Naval Museum**, in Château (40.74.53.24). *Daily, except Tue, year round.*

OUESSANT (Finistère) 18th-c. **House of Ushant Traditions** (98.48.81.92). *Daily 1 July to 30 Sep. Afternoons only from 1 Apr to 30 July, also Easter, Christmas and Feb school holidays.*

PAIMPOL (Côtes-du-Nord) **Sea Museum** (96.20.80.15). *Daily 1 Apr to 15 Sept.*
   Mad Atao schooner, *open 2-8pm from 1 June to 31 Aug.*

PEILLAC (Morbihan) **Ecomuseum** (97.91.26.76). *By appointment.*

PLEDELIAC (Côtes-du-Nord) **St. Esprit-des-Bois Farm** (96.31.14.67). *Reconstructed farm of the early 1900s. Guided tours from 1 July to 15 Sept, otherwise by request.*

PLEUDIHEN-SUR-RANCE (Côtes-du-Nord) **Apple and Cider Museum** (96.83.20.78). *Audiovisuals, tastings. Year round.*

PLÉUMEUR-BODOU (Côtes-du-Nord) **Tregor Radome and Planetarium**—Palace of Discovery: technologies of AD2000. Audiovisual display on the 20m dome.

PLOUGUERNEAU (Finistère) **Maritime**, route de St. Michel (98.04.60.30). *Daily, except Mondays, 15 June to 15 Sept. Out of season weekends and bank holidays.*

PONT-AVEN (Finistère), **Town Hall** (98.06.00.35). Exhibits of Gauguin's Pont-Aven School. *Daily, Apr to Sept.*

PONT-L'ABBÉ (Finistère) **Bigouden Museum** in the castle. *Guided visits 1 June to 30 Sept. Closed Sun and bank holidays.*
   Pays Bigouden House at Kervazegan on the road to Loctudy (98.87.35.63). *Turn-of-the-century farm reconstruction. Openings same as museum.*

PORT-LOUIS (Morbihan) **Citadel** (97.21.14.01). *Year round. Closed on Tue.*

QUEBRIAC (Ille et Valaine) **Les Brulons** collection of naturalised animals from around the world (99.68.10.22). *Daily 1 Apr to 15 Oct. Rest of the year, Sun and school holidays.*

QUIMPER (Finistère) **Beaux-Arts**, pl St. Corentin (98.95.45.20). *Daily, year round.*
School of Pont-Aven Max Jacob (98.95.04.69). *Daily, except Tue.*
Crockery, allée de Locmaria (98.90.09.36). *Mon to Fri, year round.*
Breton Departmental Museum in former bishopry, rue du Roi Gradlon (98.95.21.60). *Daily, except Tue.*

QUIMPERLÉ (Finistère) **Maison des Archers** (98.96.04.32). Archers, oyster farming and local traditions. *Guided tours on Sat mornings and afternoons. Daily, except Sun, in July and Aug.*

RENNES (Ille-et-Vilaine) **Brittany** and **Beaux Arts**, quai Émile Zola (99.79.44.16) *Daily, except Tue.*
Automobile Museum at Cesson-Sévigné (99.62.00.17). *Daily.*

ROSCOFF (Finistère) **Aquarium Charles Pérez**, pl G. Tessier (98.69.72.30). *Daily.*

ST. BRIEUC (Côtes-du-Nord) **Museum**, rue des Lycéens-Martyrs. *Daily.*

ST. GUÉNOLÉ (Finistère) **Prehistoric Museum of Finistère** (98.58.60.35). *Daily from 1 June to 30 Sept except Tue and Sun mornings.*

ST. MALO (Ille-et-Valaine) Museum in the **Château** (99.56.41.36). *Daily, except Tuesdays. In low season guided tours at 10.45, 2pm, 3.15 and 4.30.*
Quic-en-Groigne (99.40.80.26). *Daily, Easter to the end of Aug.*
Cape Horner at the Tour Solidor (99.81.66.09). *Daily, year round. Guided tours.*

ST. MARCEL (Morbihan) **Resistance Movement** (97.75.17.41). *Daily, June to Sept.*

ST. RIVOAL (Finistère) **La Maison Cornec** (98.68.87.76). Ecomuseum of Monts d'Arrée. Peasant traditions. *Daily, 1 June to 15 Sept.*

ST. THURIEN (Finistère) **Kerchuz Mill** (98.39.84.12). *Year round. Grain milled on Sun and Wed.*

STE. ANNE-D'AURAY (Morbihan) **Sacred Art** (97.57.68.80). Statuary and folklore.

SIZUN (Finistère) **House of the River, Water and Fishing**, Vergraon Mill (98.68.86.33). *Daily.*

TINTÉNIAC (Ille-et-Villaine) **Tools and Handicrafts**, quai de la Dunac. Crafts of yesteryear. *Daily, 1 July to 30 Sept.*

TRÉGARVEN (Finistère) **Rural School** (96.68.87.76). *Daily in July and Aug 2-6pm.*

TRÉGASTEL (Côtes-du-Nord) **Aquarium** (96.23.88.67). *Daily, June to Sept, until 10pm in peak season. Weekends and holidays in May.*
Prehistoric Museum. *Same opening times.*

TRÉGUIER (Côtes-du-Nord) **Renan Museum**, birthplace of Ernest Renan (96.92.45.63). *Daily except Tue and Wed from Easter to 30 Sept.*

VANNES (Morbihan) **Prehistoric** at Château Gaillard (97.42.58.80). *Year round, except Sun and bank holidays.*
Gulf and Sea (natural history), Roscanvec Hôtel, rue des Halles (97.47.24.34).
Super **Aquarium La Ferme des Marais** (97.40.67.40). *Open every day of the year.* Species from all waters. Marine biology research facilities.

Other Attractions and Activities

Son et Lumière

Châteaugiron, at the castle—*4 days at the end of June* (99.00.41.69).

Dinard, on the Promenade du Clair de Lune. *From June to Sept, Mon, Wed, Fri, Sat, and Sun* (99.46.94.12).

Vitré, reconstruction of the Middle Ages, 350 participants, 7 tableaux, 28 riders, jousting—*two weekends in June* (99.75.04.46).

Elven, King Arthur and the knights of the Round Table (97.63.79.99).

Rieux, open air theatre with 250 actors—*July and August* (99.91.90.69).

Check times and days, which can change. Entrance fees vary from 20F-40F.

Thalassotherapy Centres

Carnac, Centre de Thalassothérapie (97.52.04.44). *Year round.*

Quiberon, Institut de Thalassothérapie (97.50.19.25). *Feb to Dec.*

Perros-Guirec, Grand Hôtel, Trestraou Beach (96.23.28.97). *Year round.*

Roscoff, Ker Lena Centre (98.69.70.31). *Year round.* Institut Marin de Rockroum (98.69.72.15). *Apr-Sept.*

St. Malo, Thermes Marins, 100 bd Hébert (99.56.02.56). *Mid-Jan to mid-Dec.*

Treboul (Douarnenez), centre de Cure Marine, rue Pierre Curie (98.74.09.59). *Year round.*

Canals

Maps, guides, list of boatyards and prices from: Comité des Canaux Bretons (ABRI), 3 rue des Ports-Mordelaises, 35000 Rennes (99.31.59.44).

Walking, Cycling, Riding

Guides to the Grande Randonnée trails from Stanfords, 12 Long Acre, London WC2 (01-836 1321). For information and list of 100 hostels: ABRI, 3 rue des Ports-Mordelaises, 35000 Rennes (99.31.59.44). Information on 'Breton Ways' riding trails: ARTEB, 8 rue de la Carrière, 56120 Josselin (97.22.22.62).

Riding, biking, cycling holidays in the forest of Fougères:
La Ferme de Chenedet, Landéan 35133 (99.97.35.46).

Riding tours:
Centre Équestre de Kerneuzet, 29237 Sizun, Finistère.

Information on 29 youth hostels:
Association Bretonne des Auberges de Jeunesse, 41 rue Victor-Schoelcher, 56100 Lorient (97.37.11.65).

Golf courses

La Baule: *St. Dénac* (40.60.46.18). 18 holes. Par 72.

Belle-Île-en-Mer: *Golf de Sauzon* (97.31.64.65). New 18-hole course.

Bénodet: *L'Odet* at Clohars Fouesnant (98.57.26.16). 18 holes. Par 72. Plus 9-hole beginners' course.

Le Crouesty: *Golf du Kervert* at St. Gildas-de-Rhuys (97.45.30.09). New 18-hole course.

Dinard: *St. Briac* (99.88.32.07). 18 holes. Par 69,

Etables-Sur-Mer: *Les Ajoncs d'Or* (96.71.90.74). 18 holes. Par 72.

Missilac: *La Bretesche* (40.88.30.03). 18 holes. Par 72.

Pléhédel: *Boisgelen* (96.22.31.24). 18 holes. Par 72.

Pléumeur-Bodou: *St. Samson* (96.23.87.34). 18 holes. Par 72.

Ploemel: *St. Laurent*, 3km from Erdeven (97.56.85.18). 18 holes. Par 72.

St. Malo: *Le Tronchet*, 12km from Dinan (99.58.96.69). 18 holes. Par 71. Plus 9-hole beginners' course.

Horse-drawn Caravans

Exploring by caravan or *roulotte* is common in rural France. Each caravan is fully equipped for four people with cooking facilities.

178

Finistère: Roulottes de Bretagne, Gare de Locmaria-Berrien, 29218 Le Huelgoat (98.99.73.28).

Les Roulottes du Sud-Cornouaille, Porz an Breton, 29130 Quimperlé (98.96.16.56).

Ille-et-Vilaine: Cheval Langon Loisirs, 35660 Langon (99.08.76.42).

Morbihan: Attelages Morbinhannais, Ker Samuel, 56610 Le Saint (97.23.06.16).

INDEX

181